branding

branding

HELEN VAID

SERIES CONSULTANT
ALASTAIR CAMPBELL

WATSON-GUPTILL
PUBLICATIONS
New York

First published in the United States in 2003 by Watson-Guptill Publications, a division of VNU Business Media, Inc., 770 Broadway, New York, NY 10003
www.watsonguptill.com

The information contained in this book is given without warranty and, while every precaution has been taken in compiling the book, neither the author nor the publisher assumes any responsibility or liability whatsoever to any person or entity with respect to any errors which may exist in the book, nor for any loss of data which may occur as the result of such errors or for the efficacy or performance of any product or process described in the book.

This book was conceived, designed, and produced by The Ilex Press Ltd Cambridge England

Sales Office
The Old Candlemakers
West Street, Lewes
East Sussex
BN7 2NZ

Creative Director:
Alastair Campbell
Executive Publisher:
Sophie Collins
Art Director:
Peter Bridgewater
Editorial Director:
Steve Luck
Design Manager:
Tony Seddon
Project Editor:
Chris Middleton
Designers:
Jane and Chris Lanaway

www.designdirectories.com

A Library of Congress Cataloging-in-Publication data exists for this title

ISBN 0-8230-5682-X

Originated and printed by Hong Kong Graphics and Printing Ltd, China

All websites mentioned in this book were current at the time of writing, but due to the changing nature of the Internet, it is possible that some are now hosting different content. The author and publisher cannot accept liability for these changes and apologize for any inconvenience.

6

BRANDING—PAST AND PRESENT

Consumers who buy Calvin Klein underwear, Ford cars, or Coca-Cola without looking at competitive products are loyal to a brand. But what does this mean? One explanation is that they have internalized their purchasing to the point where it is no longer a conscious decision.

Unsurprisingly, this is the dream of every manufacturer and marketer because they believe they no longer have to invest time and money in convincing consumers to try or buy their products. Consumers believe a brand "speaks" to them in some way, and represents a lifestyle they either have or aspire to, or a unique service they want. Indeed, some people often say, "That's not my brand" when confronted by a conflicting choice.

A company's task is to maintain and manage that relationship. The brand's design (in every respect) is a signifier, even a territorial marker. But who is marking the territory—the customer or the brand owner? It's all a function of design.

According to marketers, a brand is a distinct product, service, or business, and branding is the act of impressing a product, service, or business on the mind of a consumer, or set of consumers. This process may last a lifetime, or for as long as the consumer remains in a demographic group.

Some believe that branding is not only about ubiquity, visibility, and function, but about "emotionally bonding" with a target group of customers. And a major part of that process lies in the design. So successful has some brand design been that when a consumer leaves a target age bracket, for example, they sometimes find themselves wanting to remain in it, living a young lifestyle well into middle age.

In the late 1990s and the early years of the 21st century, even state organizations and political parties have plowed huge public sums into designing brands to represent their services, usually inclusively ("Join Us" or "Use us"). Some companies, though, opt for an

"exclusive" approach by limiting their appeal to a target group, and to people who aspire to join it ("This product is for you and for people like you" or "You too can be like this"). Design is the key to making both approaches work.

Meanwhile, an opposing "No Logo" movement has sprung up in the wake of Naomi Klein's book of the same name, which explores the aggressive movements of global capital behind many lifestyle brands.

Ironically, one company—the utilitarian Japanese retailer Muji—has successfully marketed its functional, well-designed goods for urban living under the "No Brand" moniker. So in a design-conscious world full of big-name retailers, consumers can feel that they've made the "right" choice by not making the "wrong" one, and make a statement by opting out of buying an over-familiar brand. We all play the brand politics game, even if we don't want to; such is the power of even a well-designed "no brand."

MUJI
無印良品

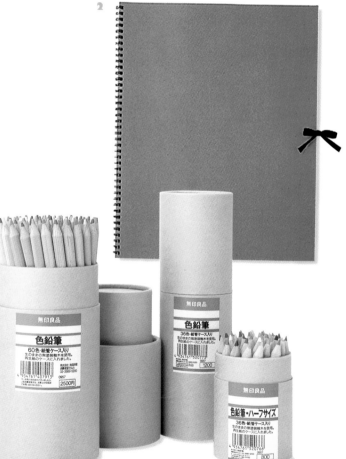

1
This sign was found carved on a tomb near the entrance of the cathedral of Uppsala, Sweden. It looks like a craftsman's cross or mark. However, it is a mark symbolizing the family of the buried man. The idea of using symbols as identifying marks has been around for much of recorded history.

2
Muji, the famous utilitarian Japanese retailer, has successfully created a brand under the "no brand" moniker.

3 | 4
Some brands such as Ford and Coca-Cola have lasted the test of time and still maintain their values and personality.

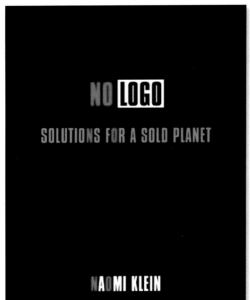

1

2

3

UK Rock band Radiohead has discovered this, too, shipping untold quantities of "unbranded" Radiohead merchandise while aligning themselves with Klein's book. It's all about good design for your target market.

But despite the arguments, branding is far from being a modern practice, even if its purpose has evolved with the rise of mass production and communication and complex social groupings. The term originated many centuries ago in the Old Norse word *brandr*, meaning "to burn." This was how farmers and owners of livestock marked their animals to identify them.

The cattle barons of the West branded their cattle territorially so that everyone could see to which ranch they belonged. In Sweden, farmers marked possessions with a family cross, which also acted as a binding signature when drawn on legal documents.

Noble families in Europe developed family crests and seals, and some went to war carrying them. These, though, were not ideograms as such, but a graphical representation of tradition and continuity in the family name. That said, the British royal family now famously refers to itself as "the Old Firm."

Today, though, even notions such as these are subject to market forces and brand positioning; think of McCartney, Coppola, Picasso, Freud… names whose mark of quality has spanned more than one generation and come to mean something new, while retaining the cachet of famous forebears.

1
Naomi Klein's book explores the aggressive movements of global capital behind many of the lifestyle brands.

2
The UK band Radiohead used the "no logo" and brand umbrella and sold large quantities of its merchandise.

3
Celebrities like Mick Jagger and Paul McCartney have created very strong personal brands apart from the brands created by groups such as The Rolling Stones and The Beatles.

4
The British royal family and suppliers of brands to them have used the endorsement of the royal crest to great effect. Brands such as Twinings have made the crest an integral part of their logo.

11

In the case of manufactured goods, in Greek and Roman times people would mark their wares with an identifiable symbol, to signal "ownership" and to establish a mark of quality. During the Middle Ages masons, stonecutters, and master builders carved their marks, just as painters began identifying their works with a signature. Over the centuries, such marks became an end in themselves as their design evolved and they came to represent not just quality or provenance, but other ideas associated with a product and, by association, its maker.

Arguably, 20th-century artists such as Andy Warhol and Damien Hirst became "brands" by the modern definition when they adopted the techniques of mass-production to make "signature," "original" goods.

5

matisse

5
Powerful signatures and brands are not just restricted to products and services; they transcend categories and industries, from fashion to art.

THE MODERN DEFINITION

The modern definition of branding developed in the 19th century during the industrial revolution when it became increasingly important for manufacturers to create identifiable names and symbols to make their products stand out from their competitors'.

As mass-production (beginning with Ford) and mass-communication networks (starting with the telegraph and the telephone) spread and gained momentum, many manufacturing brands gained the means to outlive generations and cross geographical borders. Some of those brands still exist to this day.

And as word spread, so the design of the message became as important as what the message actually said. Over time, they became one and the same thing as the brand, the logo, the aesthetic, and the "experience" became an essential means to grab market share and mindshare, and to mark out territories in both.

Today, branding is the process by which a company, a product name, or an image becomes synonymous with a set of values, aspirations, or states, such as 'youth," "independence," "trustworthiness," "quality," or "performance."

Brand equity (the value associated with a brand) is built over time through different media, such as television, radio, the Internet, print advertising, product placement (branding by association), or peer groups, particularly in the case of youth markets. When it works properly, branding results in an "autopilot" kind of purchase and the brand can become more valuable than the company (as many Internet-based ventures discovered). Brands, rightly or wrongly, can have a deep impact on their audiences' lives.

In rare instances, a brand can become synonymous with a product type. It's this power that makes many customers call adhesive tape "Scotch tape" or "Sellotape," or their vacuum cleaner a "Hoover," even if they're using competitive products. However, these territorial markers are not always permanent, particularly in fast-moving markets such as information technology and high-tech hardware.

Until recently, many office workers called their photocopiers "Xeroxes," regardless of which company actually made their machines. Indeed, "Xerox" became both a noun and a verb in common parlance, but both have fallen out of favor with a new generation, as competitors have muscled in on that company's territory. The word is now unfamiliar to many younger people, however good the company's products might still be.

1 | 2 | 3 | 4 | 5
Names like Audi, VW, Mercedes, Sony, and Budweiser are all brands with powerful associations. Each is trying to reflect a specific personality through its look, feel, and design.

"Rebranding," that often-derided term, is therefore of vital importance to many companies who have to redefine themselves around a new set of objectives—and a new design scheme to signify it.

Think of IBM: once synonymous with huge mainframe computers, then with the ("IBM compatible") PC, IBM has recently repositioned itself as a services company, with a new softer design scheme and a simplified range of product names to match. Microsoft, which once paid scant regard to the Internet, now focuses almost exclusively on it. All these new aspirations are reflected in the companies' design principles.

Question: Can you identify this company?

Not difficult! Most people can recognize McDonald's in a split second.

But why do people know McDonald's so well? The fast food market is cutthroat and crowded, and McDonald's products are broadly similar to those of its competitors, so what sets it apart? Arguably, people visit McDonald's because of the McDonald's brand, which translates into two words: "convenience" and "fun."

The company also designs many of its products and services for children, with the thinking being that if the design attracts children, kids will persuade adults to reach for their wallets. Recently, it has also pitched itself at senior citizens and ethnic minorities, and has even started poking fun at itself in TV advertisements.

McDonald's is so well established that many people look for the big yellow "M" that has come to represent the company's intended values throughout the world. A well-designed logo crosses language and cultural barriers. The colorful, welcoming brand design, which extends to packaging, uniforms, product names, and free gifts, says, "These products are fun and convenient for everyone," while its new-found sense of humor cleverly undermines its image as a corporate behemoth to attract even skeptics.

In short, McDonald's hamburgers are presold. That's the power of a brand—as long as consumers see the company in the same way that it sees itself. This is one of the inherent risks with brand positioning, and with a design that represents a company's value system. If a company's design scheme and message to consumers trumpets "trust," "innovation" or "you can talk to us," then the company had better deliver on that promise. The bigger the target, the more snipers will try to shoot holes in a company's vision of itself.

13

6

7

6 | 7 | 8
Some brands have now become so powerful that they are synonymous with their category.

8

BRANDS IN THE CONNECTED WORLD

The growth of interactive media, such as the Internet, digital and interactive TV and radio, mobile technologies, GPRS, and TiVO, has changed the rules of the branding game. Customers are willing to receive data from whichever "channel" they select and use it to make purchasing decisions, and even enter into a technology-enabled dialog with chosen suppliers. (At least, that's what many companies are aiming for, even if the technology sometimes lets them down!)

For designers today, this is the biggest challenge: is the design strategy flexible enough to maintain brand consistency across different channels and technologies? More than ever companies, which are now complex networks of partners, affiliates, and even media organizations, must establish clear guidelines for the use of their brand. These include billboards and periodical advertisements, points of sale, interactive TV and Internet portals, and the postage-stamp-sized screens and cut-down content of cellphones and mobile devices.

Branding has never been through such turbulent times—which is good news for designers. The principles of branding haven't changed, but the pace and number of potential choices have. The speed of change, the unpredictability of economies, the rapid progress of

1 | 2
The British *Financial Times* has taken its very successful newspaper brand and used similar colors and branding on the Net, enabling its customers to have the same experience across channels.

5

3

4

3 | 4
AOL have created an identity for their brand that works very well across channels, be it the Internet, PDA, or mobile.

5 | 6

The CNN logo is very
adaptable and can be
transferred across
many media and
formats without losing
any impact.

technology, and increasing market fragmentation all
conspire to make developing and managing a strong
design scheme essential.

If a consumer is buying shampoo and toothpaste,
a printer and a digital camera, or a pair of shoes and
some lingerie, the design and information requirements
are very different, and become more complicated when
the channels to deliver information are multiplying
and evolving.

Depending on whether the purchase is being made
from a catalog, on the Internet via a PC, or through
interactive TV, for example, information design
requirements have no option but to change, so the
designer must consider how to maintain brand
consistency. Navigation when shopping via interactive
TV is achieved through the remote control, so design
here must be led by simplicity. The color reproduction
possibilities of print, computer monitors, and TV are also
very different. We will examine these issues later.

So it's clear that good design is more essential than
ever to brand relevance and visibility. A strong brand
today should not only understand and adopt design
principles appropriate to the product, but also to the
channel or delivery mechanism (from business to
consumer). Brand design across new and future platforms
will play a massive role in building that visibility.

The reason for all this is that businesses think in terms
of channels, but most consumers see only the brand, and
unconnected bits of information. Customers expect all
interactions with a brand to be consistent and to provide
them with information, opportunity, and customer
service. Put simply, they want value that justifies their
time, effort, and money.

So in more and more industries, from the automobile
industry to retail banking, managing a complex
multichannel design strategy effectively and seamlessly is
a major source of competitive advantage.

15

MORE THAN JUST A PRODUCT

Recent technical advances have made speed and relevance central to success. Technology is enabling existing products, such as telephones, to converge with other technologies and delivery mechanisms. Hence we have mobile phones that can send text messages and emails, surf the Web, and which promise video, audio, and location-based services delivered in a swift and affordable form.

New delivery forms create new ways for people to interact not only with each other, but also with providers of content, such as music, film, travel opportunities, financial services, consumer goods, and groceries. Many people go so far as to join communities of users centered on content type or, more attractively for companies, content provider.

Some companies—such as Virgin —have recognized the potential in branding other companies' services, such as mobile phone networks and even electricity, and building value and additional services around them to create a community "feel."

There are challenges here for designers. As a website is a virtual megastore, the online brand presence needs to be just as tightly designed and controlled as its real-world counterpart. Increasingly, customers like to be addressed as individuals online, so sites need to be designed as "live," interactive experiences, and not just as showcases.

These changes are also influencing the types of brands that are being created for consumers. Food is no longer seen in the media as a family chore, as it was in the 1950s (for women), but as being about home and lifestyle design, and "sensory experiences" regardless of gender. To stay relevant and survive, then, it is crucial that brands understand such social, cultural, and demographic changes.

16

1

2

3

1 | 2 | 3 | 4
Depending on the brand strategy, the execution of design (regardless of the medium) changes dramatically. Apple focuses on the "must-have," unique design of its products. Amazon focuses on personalization, from greeting customers by name to recommendations based on previous purchases. Disney, on the other hand, focuses on the "experience" and fun elements, while brands like Accenture focus on their expertise and "value-adds."

5
Advertising has moved on from simply explaining the use of products to making them more experiential. The soft drinks industry, one that traditionally stressed taste, is a good example. Red Bull has pushed that concept to the next level.

Products such as computers have changed from being "technology equipment" into consumer-focused centers of "lifestyle entertainment." Airlines are less about transport and more about "travel and experience" opportunities that can augment lives through sophisticated bonus schemes such as airmiles.

But these are also rich information-gathering opportunities for the companies concerned, who are not in the free-gift business. They get something just as valuable as money in return: data about choices and lifestyles, plus the customer's repeat business (loyalty) for as long as they can maintain that relationship.

Brand design is no longer a "monologue," but a dialog between companies and customers, so businesses need to be able to shift the focus of their brands accordingly—as long as they keep the underlying principles intact.

So it's essential that designers remain at the center of this dialog, as they are responsible for designing the message and making it attractive to emerging audiences.

According to Alan Mitchell in his book, *Branding Strategies in the Information Age*, there are four new models of brand strategy that are being followed by companies today:

Relationship branding: This is where the main asset of the company is its relationship with consumers—for example, brands like Amazon and Avon. When designing brands that are relationship oriented, a designer should highlight aspects of the unique

17

relationship that a customer has with that brand. The Amazon experience is about personalizing and understanding the customer's preferences through technology channels, turning a "one-to-many" experience into a "one-to-one" dialog. Avon's, meanwhile, is still centered on direct customer contact, with precisely the same intention.

Values branding: Here the main asset of the company is its focus on a group of values, way of life, or philosophy. Examples are Disney and Nike. In these brands the design is led heavily by the values: Disney's focus is on safe, colorful, children-led family fun; Nike's is on emerging street-level trends and sporting icons to make sportswear, and sport, hip for the clubbing generation. In both cases their designs have become icons in themselves, and both have also created their own "worlds" of experience and helped define aspects of popular culture.

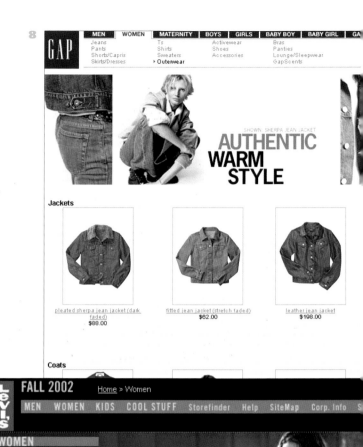

6
Avon relies on direct customer contact to maintain brand loyalty. Looking at products in your own home creates a more relaxed atmosphere.

7 | 8
Websites such as Gap and Levis try to deliver online the experience that people have in their stores, by recreating look, feel, and color choices.

9 | 10
Ferrari and Rolex
have made design and
exclusivity integral to
what the brand delivers
to its customers. Such
brands are linked with
an aspirational lifestyle.

Intellectual property branding:
Here the main asset of a company is
its specialist knowledge and know-
how, its unique approach, and range
of services. When designing for
such clients it is important that the
brand can translate such values as
knowledge, trust, professionalism,
and understanding—particularly
when customers are parting with
large sums of money to bring
onboard that specialist knowledge.
Accountancy and consultancy
giant Andersen was famously a
casualty of its promise of trust, at a
time when its branding campaign
was pushing a message of "one
company" worldwide. Not a good
time for regional headquarters to
claim that it had no knowledge
of the US office's illegal practices!
(But you can hardly blame the
designer for that.)

Passion branding: In this case the
main asset of the company is the
drive and passion that its target
customers have for the brand.
Ferrari, Jaguar, and Rolex are
obvious examples. When designing
for passion brands, understanding
the target audience is crucial. Most
people associate with these brands
on a very personal level, so the smallest "off-brand"
campaign or design can have a major impact on current
customers (who often return), and on people who
might aspire to be customers one day.

19

BRINGING BRANDS TO LIFE

Brand identity only has value when it is communicated correctly to the appropriate audience, and the views of customers are determined by what they see and hear about the brand through the media.

Brands therefore have to realize that a "scatter shot" approach (firing out untargeted messages with the hope that enough of the correct audience will be hit) no longer works. The media is no longer as simple as it was in the days when billboard, print, and, later, television advertising were the only real options. At the same time, consumers have become more sophisticated in their response to branding campaigns, just as the media has become more complex and demographically focused.

So choosing the most appropriate, targeted medium is essential for success, and design must be dictated by medium. If "Brand X" has opted to sell its products primarily via interactive TV, then having pastel shades, on the one hand, or brilliant blues and vibrant oranges on the other, will not work.

TV is limited in terms of its color palette and screen resolution, and has a problem displaying certain colors. A loud blue, for example, will often glow unattractively onscreen, and there can also be problems if blue- or green-screen processes are being used to superimpose other images, such as computer-generated backgrounds.

In some cases, the density and luminosity of certain colors has to be toned down for broadcast, so your design's color scheme will have to accommodate that in advance. Again, we will come back to these issues in future chapters.

In summary, then, it's clear that all the processes of, and considerations behind, creating a brand from scratch must be learned before creating a design blueprint. In the following chapters we will review all the elements of creating or managing a brand and how to implement these principles in the overall design scheme.

1

MOBILE

RETAIL DESIGN

PRINT & BILLBOARDS

CUSTOMER CARE

BRAND

PUBLIC RELATIONS

TV & RADIO

CORPORATE AFFAIRS

NEWS & MEDIA

1
BRAND TOUCHPOINTS
Touchpoints are important ways to create an overall brand experience. A touchpoint is wherever a customer interacts with a brand, such as its advertising, retail presence, or Internet site. The design and implementation of each of these points is part of designing a single, coherent brand.

2

3

2
British bookstore chain
W.H. Smith has created
sites on interactive TV
as well as on the
Internet appropriate
to their products.

3 | 4
Domino's Pizza
successfully uses
primary colors on its
iTV site to reflect the
"fast food" nature
of its business, while
Bertelsmann's more
refined site aims to
reflect its diverse print-
based business.

4

22

WHAT'S IN A NAME?

The name of a brand is almost always its constant element. The brand's positioning might change, its corporate colors might be adapted, the typeface modernized, and the logo revised, but few companies will ever change their name (unless the brand was designed to be ephemeral).

The only reasons for changing it might be: a merger or acquisition; a realignment of regional products under a global brand (in the case of some chocolate bars and beauty products); or a perceived need to relaunch a company with a new brand identity, or at least a modern variant. This is usually because a market has changed dramatically, as youth and technology markets are prone to do, or has vanished entirely.

In any of the above cases, renaming is still a high-risk venture in terms of how customers might react, although mergers and acquisitions are often about acquiring customers as much as they are about stock or technologies. Companies that have changed brand names, or even their own names, for any other reason are often treated with derision, or are accused of wasting money, or admitting defeat to their competitors.

When the Post Office in the UK, for example, became a "brand" under a new umbrella organization called "Consignia," there was a storm of protest and amusement from a cynical British press. The design and the branding might have been attractive enough on the surface, but commentators questioned the relevance to people who wanted to post and receive letters. Was the organization embarrassed by its own core service? Would people who relied on it know what had happened?

What this proves is that a good brand has substance, purpose, and perceived values—it does, or represents, something that people want. The strength of a good brand, then, may only come to light when a poor branding project is set against it. One that, for the sake of argument, has no obvious substance or purpose.

Of course, it's conceivable that some companies might trail new brands solely to call attention to current ones, and then "bow to public pressure" to retain the original. But whether this is true or not, never take your eyes off what your brand design represents!

Brand names play key functional roles, some of which may not be immediately obvious:

• A name is a reference point for consumers that goes beyond being something that's simply memorable. It should have far more to do with the way a customer relates (or not) to the brand. Consumers often say, "X looks like something I might buy," or "X doesn't sound like me!" In a well-designed brand, this is

Ephemeral

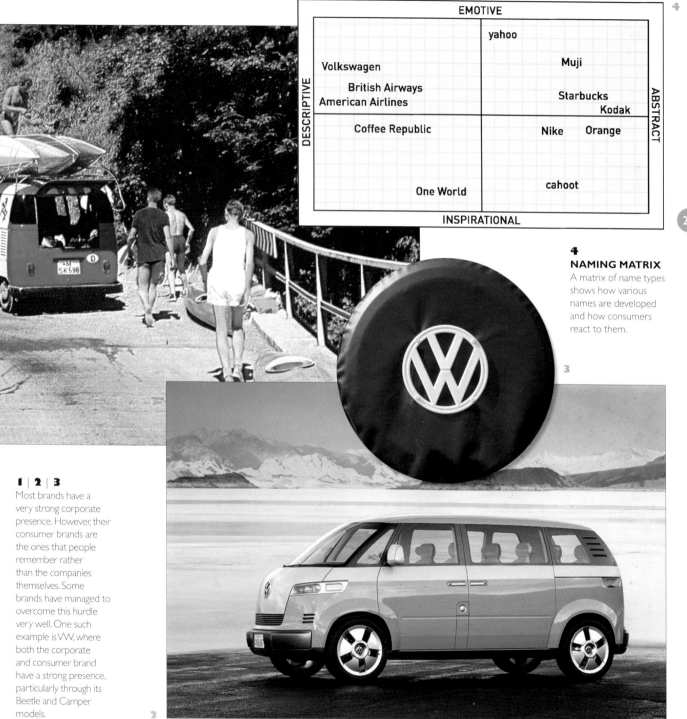

4

DESCRIPTIVE	EMOTIVE		ABSTRACT
	yahoo		
Volkswagen		Muji	
British Airways		Starbucks	
American Airlines		Kodak	
Coffee Republic		Nike Orange	
One World	cahoot		
	INSPIRATIONAL		

4
NAMING MATRIX
A matrix of name types shows how various names are developed and how consumers react to them.

3

1 | 2 | 3
Most brands have a very strong corporate presence. However, their consumer brands are the ones that people remember rather than the companies themselves. Some brands have managed to overcome this hurdle very well. One such example is VW, where both the corporate and consumer brand have a strong presence, particularly through its Beetle and Camper models.

2

WHAT'S IN A NAME? (CONT.)

deliberate: by including one set of customers, you may wish to exclude others.

• A brand name is a legal entity the company can protect—and most guard it fiercely!

• It can create value for a company as an intangible asset.

• The brand's name and visual identity also play a pivotal role in the wider marketplace: the brand must be seen and heard, not just by customers, but also by competitors.

• A name must be appropriate for the brand, appeal to the target market, and "capture" the brand in some way. It should send out a message each time it is seen, heard, discussed, or (hopefully) recalled.

The best brand names are brought to life with strong, clear, and memorable visual identities that encapsulate the brand's personality. The goal should be to engage audiences externally (the customers), but also internally (the company's employees).

This motivating aspect of a brand is often overlooked; it's a way to attract the "right" employees, keep them, and get them behind the message. Employees, like customers, should say, "That brand looks and sounds like me."

If employees don't engage with the "message," a company risks unleashing demotivated or bored employees on its customers, and no amount of strategizing, marketing, and design expertise can repair the damage. Again, if your brand promises, say, cutting-edge design and an aspirational lifestyle, then your employees had better reflect those values!

The right name also helps a company talk about itself: it defines who it is and what it does. Together with the right visual identity, it should take an unfamiliar concept and convey it as something recognizable, concrete, and desirable. Brand names and design need to articulate a single, consistent message, and, most importantly, connect with customers. Design is shorthand for the brand, reflecting its values and ambitions.

The first step in creating a brand identity is to define a naming strategy. Once defined, this should be formalized in a "naming brief" with the client.

The naming strategy includes the following:

• A description of the product and/or company. What makes it unique, different, or necessary?

• A definition of the product or company that the name must support.

• An understanding of what the name needs to convey. Is it descriptive, inspirational, emotive, or abstract, and to what extent?

• Creating a future brand architecture (a blueprint for how the brand will develop, be built on, relate to other brands within and outside the company, and be marketed).

• Identifying the target audience, plus market trends to prove the concept.

• Addressing any related language, URL, and trademark issues (more complex than they first appear!).

In marketing terms, names can be descriptive, inspirational, emotive, or abstract.

A descriptive name says what the product or company is, or does. Examples include: Rentokil, Newsweek, American Airlines, and Volkswagen ("people's car").

5 | 6
The UK airline BMI changed its name from British Midland to create a name that signified its global intentions.

5

6

1
British Airways have embodied their global nature in the design of their tail fins, while maintaining their British values and colors in the logo.

2
orange™

2 | 3 | 4
Names can play different roles for organizations. Brands can make them as close to or as far from their products as they wish. The spectrum can be seen from Orange, where the name bears no relation to the service being provided, to FedEx, which continued to keep its original roots, to Rentokil Initial.

3
FedEx®
Express

4
Rentokil Initial

An inspirational name focuses on the possibilities of the product, visualizing what the brand is aiming to achieve or evoke, for example, One World.

An emotive name suggests the "effect" of the product, such as the impact it has on people. This can be via brand values, or through imagery, and can be coined by using real words, images, or word-parts. Good examples of this include Visa (the credit card that gives you access); Benecol (derived from the Latin for good, plus "col" for cholesterol); and Esprit (the clothes chain, which aims to evoke "spirit" and "life").

An abstract name has, at first conception, no link to the product whatsoever. It can be a made-up word, or a real "freestanding," and unrelated, image. Examples, include Orange—a freestanding, real-world image; and Kodak—a made-up name.

LOGOS

A logo is the visual expression of a brand. It's a means of creating an instant, distinctive presence that can separate a brand from the competition, and allow it to develop a language of its own (including a visual one). It's a sign that communicates what the brand is about. A well-designed logo can attract its target audience, even if they are unfamiliar with the brand or are just browsing.

It's not so different from window shopping, and going into the store that looks most appealing, or picking out one product from a shelf full of similar ones. Obviously these, too, are a major part of the brand-design and identity process, as we'll explore later.

Logos are also a means of indicating origin, ownership, or association, and there are some distinct types. For example, they might take the form of a "word mark" written in a distinctive manner (such as Virgin, Coca-Cola or Coke, Surf, and Marlboro); or an abstract symbol, which may have no obvious relation to the brand name (the Mercedes star, for example, or Nike's swoosh); or it might be a hybrid of the two (the "Orange" block, with the name inside it).

Others are designed to be simple representations of a name, such as the Apple logo (which has been simplified over the years).

Sometimes logos can be pictorial in nature (such as the American Express centurion). Occasionally, the product, service, or company can "become" the logo (the Goodyear blimp, for example, McDonald's golden arches, or the Playboy bunny).

But there is method in this variety, and the choices each of these successful companies have made are exemplars of good design translating the brand's purpose or values. Apple wants to stand out from the crowd and just "be itself"—and it wants you to bite. McDonald's wants to welcome you under its overarching brand. Nike's famous symbol, meanwhile, is recognizable as a "tick" of approval.

Logos have to be updated and revised over a period of time so that they continue to convey their message correctly to the target audience. One strong consumer-facing brand continues to be Playboy.

Logos can be a useful means of condensing long company names, as in the case of United Parcel Service (UPS), or of avoiding them altogether by using a symbol or character. Examples of this include Cap Gemini Ernst & Young, and British Telecommunications. Both companies, curiously, make varied use of a faceless blue figure.

However, British Telecommunications is so confident in its use of corporate colors, typeface, and "messenger" logo that it has become better known as "British Telecom" and "BT" without any dilution of its brand presence.

Not only that, but it has radically changed its brand identity at least three times in the past twenty or so years.

3

4

5

Lucent Technologies
Bell Labs Innovations

2

vodafone

2
Both the Lucent and Vodafone logos are very similar in style, and yet consumers will have no problems in identifying which company does what. Brands can get so internalized that even small subtle differences can become very important.

3 | 4 | 5 | 6
Without explicitly stating their names or using any text, except for the telecom company BT, these brands have created very strong links with their customers. So much so, that images alone sufficiently represent the brand.

29

6

Far from demonstrating weakness, this shows just how much, and how quickly, the markets that it operates in have transformed—and it takes a confident company to rebrand itself so publicly. The "BT" logo and color scheme are now used to brand a range of separate spin-off ventures with that same corporate confidence. If these fail, or if a market collapses, the main brand will survive.

A logo, then, may be for life, or it may need to be adapted, updated, or even abandoned where the market requires a major shift of emphasis. This is a challenge to designers, who must be aware of market trends and conditions to make a meaningful contribution to any branding strategy.

BRAND TYPES

One of the first things that a designer will need to appreciate, when designing new brands or redesigning old ones, is their classification. Whether the design brief is to be "category conformist" or "category breaking," it is important to understand what the category is.

Two broad but commonly used classifications are "corporate" and "consumer" brands. Corporate brands usually relate to a company itself, such as Unilever, but can also be used broadly to describe services offered to other businesses (rather than to consumers).

Consumer brands, on the other hand, relate to the physical products or services that the company offers to its (noncorporate) customers.

In some instances corporate and consumer brands are identical. Procter and Gamble is a corporate brand, and it has major consumer brands in its portfolio, such as Pampers, Ariel, Pantene, and Pringles. The company itself, though, is not as well known as its products. But in the case of Vodafone, Sony, or Guinness, for example, the corporate and consumer brands are the same, and are equally successful.

In some cases, then, consumers know little about the corporate brand behind the familiar consumer ones. For example, they might have heard of Unilever, Procter and Gamble, VNU, EMAP, General Mills, or Ralston Purina, but they are just as likely not to have done. Usually this doesn't matter, as long as the brands in their consumer portfolios are instantly recognized and successful.

"Hidden" corporate brands in these instances are really about being known by their competitors, along with Wall Street and the City of London, and are concerned with their relative positioning. This, though, is just as important in terms of brand design and identity; corporate brands want to show themselves, and their investors, partners, advertisers, and rivals, exactly what they stand for. It's, "Look how big my portfolio is!"

Occasionally, though, one of these more hidden brands makes the mistake of assuming it is as well known by the general public as its consumer portfolio might be. This can be a costly mistake. The virtual world, for example, is littered with examples of companies who built expensive Web portals around the corporate brand, rather than their popular consumer ones, and then

1 | 2 | 3 | 4 | 5
Procter and Gamble has a consumer brand portfolio that is more widely recognized than the parent corporate brand. All the products shown here are manufactured by Procter and Gamble.

wondered why nobody visited. This has certainly been true in the publishing industry.

When designing a brand, it is vital to know what a company's real strengths are, particularly when trying to build new revenue streams around an expensive piece of design.

A more detailed classification looks at each sector or industry in more detail and classifies the types of brands by the industry they operate in—i.e., service, retail, consumer product, industrial, and commodity brands.

Service brands: In this category we are not talking about an "object," but a performance, which is much harder to design for. But in the services industry the brand takes on a very powerful role since the customer has multiple interactions with employees.

Consider the traveler at an airport. Travelers have interactions with dozens of different people as they pass from check-in through passport control to ticket-checking, and then on to board the plane, where they interact with the cabin crew, and flight attendants. All of these are design opportunities and are part of the brand "experience."

Retail brands: Retail branding is a truly unique type of branding in that it takes design to an even more experiential level. The various aspects of the interior design—graphics, layout, display systems, color schemes, fascias, signage, and even sounds and smells—all have to be considered, planned, and created for a given floor space, but still within the boundaries of the overall brand design.

BRAND TYPES (CONT.)

Consumers expect brands to deliver a specific experience; the experience of shopping at Macy's is very different from the one at Wal-Mart. Retailers also have to deal with different types of customers who come in with varying expectations.

A "time-poor, cash-rich" customer simply wants to get to what they're looking for quickly and effectively, whereas a "time-rich, cash-poor" customer will browse and enjoy a more elaborate layout. Designing effectively for such a varied group of customers is the real challenge for designers in this sector.

1 | 2 | 3 | 4 | 5 | 6
The brand experiences at British supermarket Sainsbury's and US-based Wal-Mart (*see page 164–165*) are very different. Sainsbury's concentrates on creating an enjoyable shopping experience. Wal-Mart is focused more on delivering value. These are reflected in their respective brand designs.

Consumer product brands: This is the most commonly and heavily branded business of all. Physical goods have always been associated with brands, and include many of the best-known consumer products (such as BMW, Kellogg's, Pepsi, Coca-Cola, Gillette, etc.). All are adept at communicating their brand values through design, not just of the products themselves, but of packaging, advertising, and other communications targeted at ideal customer groups.

32

2

Sainsbury's

Industrial product brands: A lot of products are meant for business, as opposed to consumer, usage. These brands and their designs are very different from consumer brands. Most "business-to-business" (B2B) brands have a diverse purchasing cycle and process, so traditional techniques of designing, naming, and creating "experiences" need to be modified to suit the customer base across every channel that is used to reach it.

Commodity brands: In recent years there has been an increased tendency to brand commodity goods. (A commodity is a product so basic that it cannot be physically differentiated in the minds of the consumer.) With commodity products it is hard to create brand loyalty, as the company is not providing a unique product or service. Brand designs in this sector, therefore, are moving toward representing a "mark of quality." Some examples of branded commodities are orange juice (Del Monte), oatmeal (Quaker), bananas (Chiquita), and so on.

Branded products risk becoming increasingly generic as customers stop visualizing the differences between them. This is when design differentiation becomes even more important.

Some of the areas that have now become largely undifferentiated are: consumer services (such as Visa and MasterCard); "e-tailing" and Web reference sites (such as Pets.com and PetsMart.com; Maps.com and MapQuest.com); consumer goods (especially hair and beauty products); and catalog clothing brands.

33

BRAND POSITIONING—THE KEY TO SUCCESS

Understanding the brand's "positioning statement" (its blueprint of what it is, what it represents, and where it is going) helps designers to interpret the brand's personality.

Brand positioning is the promise that a brand makes and delivers to its customers. This is not set in stone, because as most consumers know, brands often chase or set the whims of fashion. The brand's focus, emphasis, and benefits can be amended or changed over time.

Companies often position their brands differently for different times, but the underlying "mission," in business jargon, should never change. A mission is what a company thinks is wrong with the world, and what it's going to do to fix it.

Together, a company's vision, mission, commercial ambition, and values are central to any brand. Brand design should represent these, while appealing to the target customer and setting the product apart in the market. A difficult balancing act.

It's clear that positioning is very much a real-time, people-intensive effort. It helps define who and what a company is, and what it does. It explains where a company fits into the marketplace, what it has to offer that is unique—and why people should care. The designer's job is to make these concepts concrete

and appealing. Customers want to know exactly what's in it for them.

IBM's recent success in rebranding itself as a friendly, professional services company was achieved by targeting board-level executives. To IBM, chief executives, chief information officers, and chief finance officers are the people who hold the purse strings of multimillion-dollar technology-buying decisions.

IBM decided to speak directly to the decision maker faced with conflicting advice from internal teams. The approach was simple and effective: "You can trust us to solve your problem. We're IBM. We understand all this complicated stuff." The rebranding, though, played to a wider consumer audience on national TV as part of its "reassuring" message, as well as to the business press.

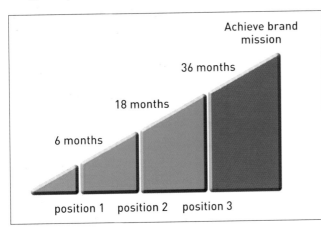

1
BRAND MISSION
It takes time for a product or company to achieve its brand mission. On average, models have shown that it takes about 6 years before a brand is really well established.

2 | 3
IBM has successfully rebranded itself as a friendly professional services company.

Now you hav
anytime, any
Intel® Pentiu

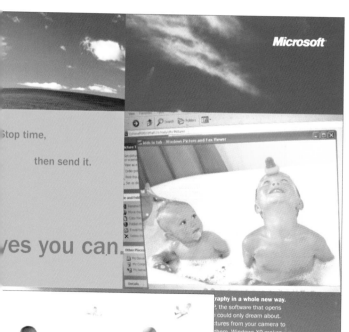

Stop time,

then send it.

ves you can.

Go mobile.

35

Another IT company, Oracle, is concentrating on its corporate brands. Oracle's effort has focused on casting itself as the e-business software provider of choice. Again, its rebranding has targeted business, but through the broader channels of billboards and advertisements in the national and business press.

Out of necessity, Microsoft's branding strategy has been more diffuse. First, it needs to keep its grip on the slowing PC market. However, Microsoft is saying to businesses that it lies at the heart of the Internet and Web-related services with its new ".Net" initiative. Meanwhile, it is also playing a youth lifestyle card by focusing on the gaming market with the XBox.

Mergers and acquisitions have wide-reaching brand-positioning implications. When Ciba-Geigy and Sandoz merged they had to create a new name, identity, and positioning to reflect the new organization. That brand is Novartis.

On other occasions, individual brands can be strengthened when two companies merge, or one acquires the other. When Ford bought Jaguar, for example, the reliability of Jaguar cars increased to higher levels, while the line brand maintained its reputation for styling, elegance, and power.

6

7

4
The "Intel Inside" campaign is a good example of positioning being in sync with brand. The proposition that a PC performs better with an Intel chip is a branding campaign that can run alongside any PC manufacturer's own.

5 | 6 | 7
Each of these Microsoft products has managed to create a compelling brand in the category in which it operates.

4

5

BRAND PERSONALITY

While brand positioning focuses on what the brand can do for the customer, brand personality concentrates on what the brand says about the customer, and how the customer feels about that.

Brand personality is what communicates the brand proposition to its target audience, and a large part of that process is design led. It does not refer to the personality of the consumers. Rather, it's designed to be a personality that attracts the right people. For example, the Virgin brand is designed to be fun, wacky, impulsive, and irreverent. This has to come across visually in everything the brand does.

Designers should ask the following questions:
• If brand X were a person, what sort of person would it be?
• If brand X were a person, what would his or her hobbies be? What kind of clothes would he or she wear? What kind of sports would he or she play?
• If brand X were a house, what kind of house would it be?
• What is the first thing that comes into your mind when you think of brand X?

Alternatively, designers can approach it in a "complete the following sentence" style. "People like brand X because…" These are valuable exercises.

Next, designers must decide whether status and lifestyle are important to the brand. Brand personality always has a self-expressive function, if only by association. People don't buy a Mercedes just because of the car's performance. They buy because of the perceived status and lifestyle that the brand represents. They pay to adopt the brand's personality, or to be seen associating with it.

Commodity and service-oriented personalities tend to be less glamorous and exciting. In fact, Surf, Colgate, Tide, Andrex, and so on, tend to develop personalities "on top of" the product. Often they will create an appealing character—usually an anonymous, but instantly recognizable one, such as the Andrex puppy.

1 | 2
Luxury and lifestyle brands, such as Boss, Prada, and Calvin Klein, have all created an image of excellence based on good quality and superior design. Another brand that has used its image well is The Body Shop, whose products sell partly because of the ethical principles reflected in its branding.

This gives their products a greater presence, and customers appreciate companies' efforts to make their brands more "friendly."

Appliance brands are often considered personality-free. They have a commodity identity. But in research carried out by Whirlpool, the washing machine company found that its brand was regarded as having a gentle, feminine personality, thanks in part to the discreet design scheme.

"Masculine," "feminine," or "caring" personalities might be applicable to many brands, but research of this nature risks being flawed by being carried out by the manufacturers themselves. That said, such research is an acceptable part of a branding exercise. It's always good to find out what customers think—especially if they agree or disagree with the way a brand sees itself.

3 | 4
Companies often create a "character" to personify the personality of the brand. Andrex and Pringles—even though in very different categories—have done just that.

BRAND PERSONALITY (CONT.)

Brand personalities, even in the household goods and appliances market, are design opportunities, and a good way of subtly differentiating brands in the market. But there should be a note of caution. Brands must be careful about suggesting that "women choose the household's washing machine," for example, or that "our machines remind unreconstructed men of their mothers"!

These are genuine social, political, cultural, and gender issues that every brand has to take onboard, especially when pitching at a household market.

In his book, *Romancing the Brand*, David Martin maintains, "Great brands are built over long periods of time with advertising that is faithful to product personality... Brand personality is permanent. Lose it and lose the franchise."

Certainly, brands such as McDonald's, Mercedes, Wal-Mart, and Virgin all have personalities that have remained the same for many years. However, there are brands that have managed to evolve not only their positioning, but also their personalities and their values, successfully.

One such example is the UK glucose drink Lucozade. Starting out as a downbeat, medicinal brand associated with recovering from illness, it has repositioned itself as a trendy, sporty lifestyle brand.

Lucozade has brought onboard popular figures, from British soccer player Michael Owen to gaming icon Lara Croft, to become "faces" of the brand. It's a clever strategy, as such figures have a cross-generational following, but with an accent on youth. By doing this,

38

1 | 2
The Jolly Green Giant, Pillsbury doughboy, Baby-Bel cows, and Fairy Liquid baby are examples of characters that attempt to give a personality to commodity-type products. One character, though—Captain Bird's Eye—has been completely reimagined to attract the youth market.

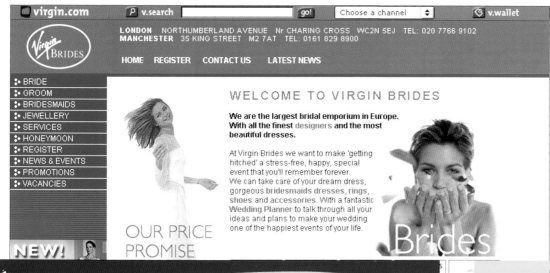

4

Lucozade has expanded its customer base, but not alienated any particular group of users.

Another recent example is one of the largest mobile operators in the UK, One 2 One. In 2002, it rebranded itself as T-mobile. The company said, "...the new personality of our brand is confidence—something One 2 One didn't have."

Designers must be aware whether a brand's essential personality is to be changed, or just its relative positioning in the market.

3 | 4
Virgin cosmetics, Virgin Megastores, Virgin Trains, Virgin Mobile, and Virgin Bride all reflect the central values of the monolithic Virgin brand. These are value for money, quality, service, fun, and innovation.

2

BRAND ARCHITECTURE

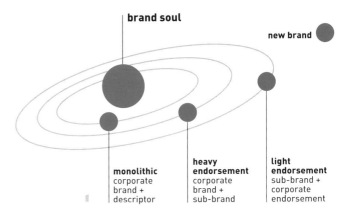

Most large companies start off with one brand, and after years of acquisition and growth end up with several in their portfolio. But what they often fail to think about are the design implications and costs of keeping all these brands effective in the marketplace.

Brand architecture is the implementation of a brand portfolio. Most commonly it defines the relationship between corporate brands and sub- (or spin-off) brands, or a corporate brand and its main products and services.

There are four main types of brand architecture. It is important to understand these, because each has rules that have a major impact on design.

Monolithic: The brand reins supreme, and products and services are simply given names that relate to the main brand, as in the case of Virgin's products and services. This means designers are very restricted as to what can or can't be done every time a new sub-brand is launched, as it has to be designed in line with the parent brand.

Heavy endorsement: A strong sub-brand stands alongside a strong parent. Perhaps the best examples are automobiles, where branding is usually based on model line, such as Toyota Celica, Toyota Supra, and Toyota Corolla. When designing a new brand, designers have to be aware of the importance of the main brand, but cannot make the parent brand too strong when it comes to the "look and feel" of the sub-brand.

Light endorsement: The parent brand takes a lesser role and acts purely as a support to the sub-brand. One example is Smirnoff Ice, the "ready to drink" or RTD, a stand-alone brand from Smirnoff vodka.

New brand: There is no relationship with the parent brand. For example, when online banking service egg was launched in the UK, it was intentionally kept separate from its parent, the insurance giant Prudential. This allowed an entirely new design scheme and personality to be created.

40

1
A MODEL FOR BRAND ARCHITECTURE
By understanding the brand soul at the heart of a company's long-term brand strategy, we can plot the relationship between the brand and its sub-brands.

2
When entering the alcopops category, Smirnoff created very heavily endorsed sub-brands to capitalize on the value of the parent brand in the vodka category.

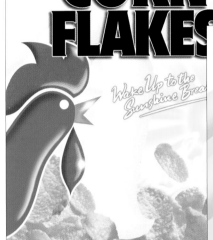

41

3 | 4 | 5 | 6 | 7 | 8
Kellogg's have kept a very strong parent brand, but created equally strong sub-brands to develop a broader presence in the very competitive cereal market.

9 | 10
Some brands are created to be distinctly different from the parent brand because the identity being created does not share all of the parent brand's values, or is trying to appeal to a different set of customers. One such brand is egg, whose parent Prudential kept egg distinctly different.

BRAND MANAGEMENT

Once the brand architecture has been clarified, the brand design needs to be managed over time to reflect changes in market conditions and fashion.

Managing the values of a brand as it moves from growth to maturity is very important, especially as the speed of change in design accelerates. Most brands need to stay fresh, and all need to stay relevant; and these are crucial tests for their design.

Over the last few decades there have been major shifts in the way companies conduct brand management. The focus has shifted from local industry to the global market that brands operate in. This is a change from one-off tactical measures to broader strategic thinking.

Today, strategic thinking represents a move toward "think global, and act local"; a shift from product management to category management; and a switch from product branding to corporate branding.

Allied with this is a closer focus on customer relationships, rather than pushing a brand indiscriminately. All of this adds up to managing a brand's equity, and that requires a strong relationship between brand and customer.

Managing brands over time is a tough challenge for any brand and its designers. It requires a long-term view of all marketing and design decisions. Sometimes one or more elements of a brand have to be changed to maintain its value in prevailing market conditions.

A "listening" financial service brand, in particular, must alter its focus radically for an economic downturn and for an upswing. In a downturn, the brand design and message might say, "We can help you protect and manage your finances." In an upswing, the focus might be, "We can help you grow your investments and take new opportunities." But the underlying values of the brand remain the same.

On occasion, a company will listen to such an extent that the customers end up calling the shots. Federal

42

1 | 2
DFW Airport has an online guide with instructions for all vendors, merchants, and service personnel on the proper use of corporate logos and IDs. This is to ensure that all partners apply the logo and branding correctly in their designs.

3
General Electric publishes its brand standards online. The site provides reference materials on the proper use of the GE monogram, plus global navigation bars and detailed specifications.

or Graphics and Pictures

- All Types | Guidelines for Headlines | Guidelines for Stories | Guidelines for Mixed
cs and Pictures

1 Include the latest Reuters logo (solid, non-dotted typeface) and display it near the top of page. It must be at least 164 x 41 pixels in size and can link to http:// www.reuters.com

2 Display correct headline crediting, as supplied by Reuters

3 Provide clearly visible written credit to Reuters and to any photographer credited in

4 Reuters has created online branding guidelines, which are aimed at its partners and are also available to the public. The site enables users to understand the proper use of page layouts, IDs, and corporate trademarks.

5 In an attempt to communicate a healthier image, Kentucky Fried Chicken's name was truncated to KFC. The company also introduced a new logo incorporating the character symbol of Colonel Sanders as a means to maintain tradition, while updating his appeal.

Do's:

Provide more than just guidelines. These can be provided as downloadable templates, style sheets, images, code, or any other material that improves the utility of the brand management site.

Always keep it simple. The aim is to make the difficult task of following brand standards much easier.

Always keep it updated. There is nothing worse than out-of-date guidelines, or a website that has not been updated.

Don'ts:

Just post a document. Simply providing a document describing your brand standards is not enough. You have to provide working examples and templates.

Ignore users. Simple Web-tracking tools or user registration windows can help companies understand who is using the website and what assets they are downloading.

Think the job is over. Effective brand management is an ongoing task. Web-based systems and tools are designed merely to overcome some of the inefficiencies of the marketing process.

Express, for example, knew that everyone called it "FedEx." So it accepted the fact and changed its name. FedEx was born, and a new logo and design scheme were introduced. This did nothing to damage the brand; rather, it strengthened FedEx's relationships with its customers, who felt a sense of "ownership" of the move.

Similar moves have been made over the years by periodicals, for example, which have abbreviated their names and taken the opportunity to develop simpler, more eye-catching designs that attract attention on the newsstand. Periodicals live or die by maintaining their readership communities.

One commonly used method of brand management, especially for franchise brands, is posting the brand standards on the Internet. Here are some hints and tips.

LIVING THE BRAND—BRAND EXPERIENCE

Many companies spend millions of dollars converting prospects into customers, only to lose their loyalty to competitors. What can a brand designer do to stop this and minimize what, in business jargon, is known as "customer churn"?

The answer lies in understanding first the experience that a customer has—or does not have—of a particular brand. This requires a sophisticated understanding of the "touchpoints" that a brand has with its customers (*see* page 20). A touchpoint is any point at which a customer comes into contact with the brand. The various touchpoints might influence them positively or negatively.

Whether it is the retail store, the bank statement sent through the mail, the TV advertisement, the billboard on the road, or even the customer service person on the telephone, each of these touchpoints leaves a strong impression on the customer. We will review and analyze these in more detail in Chapter 4.

Understanding the concept of touchpoints underpins a strong brand strategy—one that can rise above day-to-day market pressures. Many customers today look to experience something unique and special about their brand—partly, it must be said, because their brand's competitors will provide it if their brand does not. Every new design scheme, service, or "value add" raises the stakes in a competitive game. However, customers have also become media savvy and skeptical, so the promise must deliver something concrete.

Designs must translate brand values into a real experience, from the product all the way through to the in-store experience or its virtual equivalent, via the logo, color scheme, uniform, and service culture.

Starbucks invented its own language for its products, and thereby enhanced both its brand design and the experience of consuming its goods.

44

BE UNFORGETTABLE™

INTRODUCING REVLON° TEES
A whole new way to wear Revlon®. Sold exclusively at Fred Segal Santa Mon So what's your color? >>

TEN MINUTES TO BEAUTIFUL HAIR

DIE ANOTHER DAY
James Bond is back in Die Another Day,

2

One brand that has managed what it stands for across eras and continents is Revlon. Charles Revson, of Revlon, famously said, "We are not in the business of selling cosmetics, we are in the business of selling hope."

45

3

3 | 4

Borders has changed the rules of retailing by creating an environment that encourages browsing, and which enhances the experience of buying books and CDs, via add-ons such as in-house coffee shops and live performances.

4

46

KEY ELEMENTS OF BRANDING

A clear design strategy helps influence people's perception of a brand in such a way that they are persuaded to act in a certain fashion. For example, consumers might be persuaded to buy and use the products and services, purchase at higher price points, or donate to a cause. As branding is typically undertaken in a competitive environment, the aim is to persuade people to prefer the brand over the competition.

Understanding the crucial elements of branding is vital for a designer. It helps bring a brand's values to life.

The design elements of branding are:

• **Experiential**: How should the buyer feel when he or she purchases the product or service? How should this be communicated in the design?

• **Functional**: What benefit does this brand provide to the buyer? How can this be communicated in the design? And should this be done directly or implicitly?

• **Emotional**: How would we like the customer to feel about owning this brand? And how will he or she actually feel, given our chosen design strategy?

• **Rational**: Alternatively, will this brand appeal to the logical side of our buyer? Is this what we want? And how can this be communicated in the design?

• **Cultural**: Is there a culture of buying this brand? Among whom? Why? Does the brand reflect this? Or does the culture of buying it reflect the brand?

• **Visual**: What should this brand look like? And why? Elements here include color, typography, logo, and packaging. How will these appeal to the target market?

We read a brand's values according to the way they are presented to us visually. Alternatively, a brand's visual identity can come to represent values that have been communicated to us by other means. In either case, colors, names, logos, and typefaces are what we see and register first. They become a symbol of the brand and its associations for us.

To its devotees, the Nike "swoosh" stands not for a brand, but for an aspiration to be the best or to excel in whatever they do. Nike is an example of how persuasive a branding strategy can become when it is well executed.

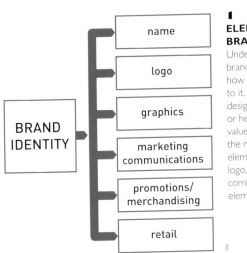

ELEMENTS OF BRANDING

Understanding what a brand is or does, and how people will react to it, is crucial for a designer as it helps him or her bring brand values to life through the most appropriate elements (e.g., name, logo, graphics, etc.) or combinations of elements.

 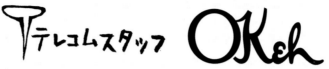  

49

2
All these music brands
are owned by the
Japanese electronics
and music giant Sony.
Each brand has been
designed to reflect the
music produced for
that label.

COLORS MAKE A DIFFERENCE

Companies spend millions of dollars building brands that have distinctive colors, especially when it comes to their packaging. Instant recognition of a world-class brand is what many companies seek from intelligent use of this global visual language.

Where possible, manufacturers like their brands to "own" colors, even when a color has come to represent a type of product through universal adoption. Red has been widely adopted by soft drink companies, for example, especially for "cola" drinks.

Coca-Cola is the preeminent example, and despite numerous own brand and big-name versions of cola-style drinks, Coca-Cola can regard itself as the progenitor of the Cola red. Arguably, "own-brand" versions reinforce Coca-Cola's solid visual identity.

Coke's main rival, Pepsi Cola, moved against the category benchmark and adopted blue, lifting itself above the plethora of own-brand copycats, and setting itself apart from its competitor.

Turquoise is seldom associated with foodstuffs, but Heinz has made it synonymous with its famous brand of baked beans. Shell's yellow, Cadbury's purple, and Heineken's green all represent different values to different customers.

1 | 2 | 3 | 4
The colors shown here have come to represent brands, to the extent that these brands now own the category and color combination—whether it's Coke's red, Heineken's green, or Pepsi's blue.

Other prominent brand identities that are associated with specific colors include many cigarette brands, some of which have sidestepped public disquiet about images of smoking in tobacco advertising through clever campaigns that have concentrated on the brand's color identity, rather than the product.

Consumers today have become so used to color coding within products' ranges that they expect them, and any change leads to confusion and conflict. And that means bad publicity.

50

A classic case of this was Walkers', a British snack company's, salt and vinegar potato chips. Traditionally, salt and vinegar chips from several manufacturers used to "own" the color blue—it was a useful "sku" (stock-keeping unit). Then Walkers decided to put them into green packets. The move created confusion at first. Green had until that time been the color most associated with the popular cheese and onion flavor, but the tactic worked and sales rose.

Gordon's distinctive green became the benchmark for gin bottling. However, this presented an opportunity to its competitor, Bombay Sapphire. Its bottles' blue-tinted glass makes the gin look blue, and this formerly "traditional" brand seem more modern.

51

'e tastes good

WWW.PEPSIONE.COM

ONE

COLORS MAKE A DIFFERENCE (CONT.)

In conjunction with shape, color can create winning brands when used creatively, as the Perrier bottle demonstrates. Category-breaking colors in particular can create an enormous impact for a brand, such as when Heinz changed the color of its tomato sauce to green, garnering enormous publicity.

A number of brands are now primarily associated with a color, even though that color was never intended to be used as a branding issue. A good example is Yellow Pages. When its directories were first made yellow, the reason was simple: to maintain the attention levels of bored or sleepy operators. Today the color is an integral part of what the brand is about.

Yellow Pages has since made clever use of its color and its rather prosaic name with spin-off ventures such as Yell (www.yell.com), the online service that you call for help.

But brands have to be cautious about the cultural and international significance of certain colors. In parts of Southeast Asia, for example, black is seen as the color of death (as it is worldwide, of course, but there the use of the color is taken far more seriously). Many corporate Internet sites are designed with a black background, or feature the color very heavily. The Internet is a global medium, so it is always worth bearing in mind potential regional sensitivities.

1 | 2
Heinz has managed to use a nonfood color to represent the category of baked beans and have made it synonymous with the category. Meanwhile Orange, the mobile company, has made the color orange its own.

Business is turning to Orange

With over 13 million customers, including a third of the FTSE top 100 companies, Orange is now Britain's largest mobile network. And with a network already covering 123 countries and business operations in 22 countries, we are continuing to expand our global footprint. Whatever the nature of your business and wherever it takes you, for complete wirefree™ communications solutions turn to Orange.

For more information call Orange Business Solutions on 0800 037 33 37 or visit www.orange.co.uk/business

N.B. FTSE 100 companies include the listed company or subsidiaries.

orange

1

2

3 | 4 | 5 | 6
Colors have come
to characterize
categories. Shell's
yellow, Cadbury's
purple, Gordon's green,
and the variety of
colors the British
snack company,
Walkers, uses to
define the various
flavors of its chips
are all examples of
that fact.

53

3

4

5

6

TYPOGRAPHY

Imagine we are creating a new label for a clothes' range for the 16–25 women's market. The audience is in the ABC1 demographic group, with a high disposable income. They wear fashionable clothes, changing with each season. Let's say that the company has decided to call the brand "Marissa." The typeface creates the personality of this brand and each of those shown opposite signals a very different character.

Example A speaks more to the little girl inside the maturing adult: it's "girly" and flashy, suggesting a downmarket product that's not sufficiently ironic to have a trash aesthetic.

Example B is discreet, feminine, and chic, suggesting something aspirational, yet mature and adult: a mark of classic quality to aim for.

Example C speaks to a trendy, club-culture audience, to girls who buy more "left-field" style periodicals, and who live for music, friends, weekends—and the moment.

Any brand designer has to understand the market, the design brief, and the implications of getting it wrong. Consumers from all demographic and cultural groups are all willing players in the design game. They know what is aimed at them, and what is wrong for their market and for their demographic group.

Young people especially can spot a fake, and brands that aspire to speak their language will be dead in the water if they get it wrong. This is especially true when peer pressure from friends raises the stakes even higher to be seen with the "right" brands.

The product might be good, but is the label "wrong"? And does the name "Marissa" work as well conceptually, when it is set in each of the above typefaces?

Typographic styles control the image of the brand by giving it an instant disposition. Many strong, monolithic brands have built their identities on the back of good typography, matched by a product and service culture that displays the brand's values.

54

A

Each of these fonts creates a very different personality for the brand "Marissa."

ssa ^BMARISSA

^C Marissa

55

RISSA

sa MARISSA

1
Typography, and the use of photography, reflect the personality and create the voice for periodicals on the newsstand.

Industries in which typography plays a vital role are typically where the customer's interface with a brand is very intimate, such as fashion, beauty, and periodical publishing. Lifestyle periodicals such as *Cosmopolitan, Vogue, GQ,* and *Maxim* communicate very different values through their visuals, particularly their "mastheads"—how the title is typeset. This is so that, on a crowded newsstand, the brand can speak to its target readers quickly and draw their attention away from competitive products.

Cover design is the be-all and end-all of brand design in publishing: a cover can make or break an issue, and sometimes even a periodical. Sales figures and advertising statistics are sliced and diced in minute detail to see whose face shifted the most units. Statistics like these can create an A-list and a B-list of celebrity media power, and these often say far more about a star's popularity than their salary packages.

Some brands have used unique typography to create visual signatures for themselves. These brands are especially common in the fashion world. Chanel's interlocking Cs; the superimposed L & V for Louis Vuitton; the CK of Calvin Klein. All are powerful visual signals that communicate with customers, and some—such as Louis Vuitton—become sought after in their own right as symbols that customers use to make a statement about themselves.

2

2
Fashion brands try to develop signatures that can act as their marks across a variety of products, merchandise, and new product developments. Chanel's intertwined double C acts as a powerful visual reminder of the brand. Designing the right logo for such brands is fraught with difficulties.

3
Periodicals such as
Allure, *Wired*, and
Cosmopolitan have
all built strong
identities through their
typography and use
of images. Brands like
these are easy to
identify in the
newsstands and attract
a target audience.

LOGOS—THE KEY VISUAL

Logos are by far the most powerful and familiar visual expressions of a brand. Logos denote the business visually, and link brands with their historical predecessors (as we discussed throughout Chapter 1). Ultimately, logos should capture and translate the company's values and mission. When customers see a logo, they should know not just who it represents, but what.

The process of designing a logo should start with the setting of objectives and a description of what the logo ought to "say." These form the design attributes that will be portrayed in the new logo, and are usually mapped out by the brand strategist before being passed to the designer. Intent has to be articulated before design begins.

Once the intent is clear, then ideas for representing the newly established brand values are often displayed visually on "mood boards." These are tested either internally or externally to find the best match for the brand.

One brand whose logo and visual identity have been kept fluid in recent years, to depict both its

international stature and the shifting nature of the travel market, is British Airways.

Another example of a recently updated and refreshed identity is that of British Petroleum (BP). In 1998, BP and Amoco merged to form BP Amoco. Subsequent acquisitions of ARCO and Castrol resulted in a company with over 100,000 employees in 100 countries.

1 | 2
Reflecting a consistent image by using the logo in a standardized manner is key for all retail brands. Here specific instructions have been given for the typography, coloration, and positional guides. Even a presentation bottle to celebrate the pop star Kylie Minogue has the same design parameters applied.

2

MARKING UP OF THE EVIAN LOGO FOR PACKS

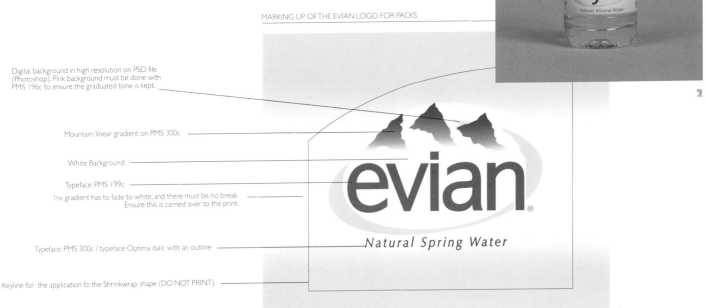

Digital background in high resolution on PSD file (Photoshop). Pink background must be done with PMS 196c to ensure the graduated tone is kept.

Mountain: linear gradient on PMS 300c

White Background

Typeface: PMS 199c

The gradient has to fade to white, and there must be no break. Ensure this is carried over to the print.

Typeface: PMS 300c / typeface Optima italic with an outline

Keyline for the application fo the Shrinkwrap shape (DO NOT PRINT)

1

58

3
Many brands now have different versions of their logos and other symbols. Nestlé uses various logos for its different "need" categories. In the ultra-fresh food sector it uses the former Chambourcy logo (birds in their nest). It uses another for chocolate, and yet another for cereals.

4
BP wanted a logo and design scheme that embodied the attributes BP wanted to possess and project to its customers and partners—the green and the flower shape say "environmentally friendly."

The new organization needed an identity that would stand for its hard-won leadership position. BP wanted a logo and design scheme that would personify the attributes it sought to possess and project to its customers and partners. These were performance, environmental leadership, innovation, and progressive thinking.

Brand consultancy Landor was asked to develop a new identity to reflect BP's aspirations. Landor suggested that the name BP held a lot of brand equity and should be kept, and that the company should become a single global brand.

The *helios* (meaning "sun") mark that was developed symbolized the newly merged company. Bright and bold, the identity was intended to position BP as an environmental leader, and help the company achieve its goal of moving beyond the petroleum sector.

STRUCTURAL CHANGE—MAKING A DIFFERENCE

In many sectors, such as FMCG (fast-moving consumer goods)—which includes items such as food, drink, pharmaceuticals, and beauty products—packaging is a key brand differentiator. Packaging not only makes a strong brand statement on overstocked shelves, but it also creates merchandising opportunities.

Perrier, Absolut, Jack Daniels, Evian, and other drink brands use bottle shapes to make a distinctive statement. In the canned drinks market, where there are fewer opportunities to use different shapes, graphics are the most important element.

Even teabag companies experiment with shapes and product designs. Whether it is pyramid bags, round ones, individually wrapped sachets, or drawstrings that squeeze out every last drop, each makes a strong statement, aiming for brand loyalty and an emotional response.

Usually, the real benefits are to the brand, although many commodity innovations are sold on the back of benefiting the customer. Familiarity and originality are the names of the game. Marmite's jar, Jif's plastic lemon, Grolsch's lager bottle (the stopper from which became a fashion accessory in the 1980s!), and Toblerone's famous pyramid shape are all examples of structures that appeal, without promising any functional advantage.

Technical advances, particularly in materials and manufacturing processes, make it easier to experiment with inexpensive and innovative package designs. These have environmental benefits when they are made with biodegradable materials. And they can have unexpected benefits, too, such as the successful "missing persons" project on milk cartons.

And the technical advances don't end there. Designers are increasingly taking advantage of techniques originally developed for architectural drafting and computer-aided manufacturing to test the viability of 3D concepts.

One area where innovative packaging design has been a key motivator is the fragrance industry. For example, the Kenzo fragrance for men, "Zebra," has simulated zebra hair on the cap, while the Boucheron Jaipur bottle is modeled as a bracelet. Perhaps even better known are Gaultier's male and female fragrances. These are sold in elegant, if slightly kitsch, bottles modeled on well-toned male and female bodies. This is a perfect example of the medium and the message being one and the same thing, and it's a message that appeals to Gaultier's target audience of young, independent men and women who appreciate his sense of camp.

1

1 | 2 | 3 | 4
Absolut, Gaultier fragrances, Marmite, and Toblerone are all examples of unique structures and shapes that have created a strong brand identity.

5
The most well-known example of a brand translated through its packaging is the Coca-Cola bottle. It was launched in 1916 in the US and is the most familiar pack shape in the world. In the shape of the bottle lies much of the equity of the brand.

2

5

3

4

USING FUNCTIONAL CAPABILITIES

Many brands appeal to customers because they have a very clear purpose. That purpose makes the brand not only unique, but also easier to position, maintain, and design for. For consumers, the reason to buy such a product is that it "does what it says it will do." It's a purchase based on need, or precaution.

Security is one sector that is characterized by functional brands. Many security brands have won a reputation for quality and reliability over the years. Consumers frequently err on the side of caution by choosing familiar names, some of which have been in the business for generations.

Brands like Yale and Banham have built customers' trust over long periods of time. Chubb, for example, started with mortise locks, and has since diversified into a range of professional, domestic, and even fire-prevention security products. The company has even identified complementary markets such as insurance into which it can transfer its considerable brand equity.

If you have a break-in, you change the locks or blame yourself; you rarely blame the lock maker. If your house keys say "Yale" or "Chubb" on them, you will still associate securing your home with these hefty brands' products, even if you didn't buy them yourself.

Brands like these rarely shout their wares from the rooftops with flashy designs, eye-catching logos, or innovative packaging. They don't need to; security products, such as locks, aren't something that people buy

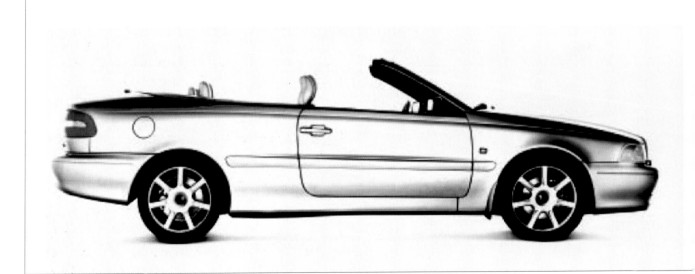

Life is too short to worry about your insurance.

» CHUBB COMMERCIAL INSURANCE
» CHUBB SPECIALTY INSURANCE
» CHUBB PERSONAL INSURANCE

C
CHUBB

For more information, consult your independent
agent, or visit us at www.chubb.com and click on
"Find an agent."

VOLVO
for life

1
A recent Chubb
advertising campaign
stressed its "worry-
free" philosophy. "Peace
of mind" is what Chubb
offers potential US
commercial and
personal insurance
customers.

2
From styling disaster to
being one of the safest
cars was a natural shift
for Volvo to make. The
company has reflected
this not only in the
design of its new
models, but also in
its advertising and
branding campaigns.

every day, but they are something that everyone needs. A designer's brief here would be simply to maintain, and possibly build on, such companies' reputations for functional, reliable products.

The automobile market is another difficult one, as most people purchase automobiles based on reputation and image. While this might be seen as a plus-point for the industry's big-budget branding exercises, people tend to stay loyal to brands, making it difficult to persuade them to change (unless they have moved into a higher income bracket).

The key to successful branding in this market is to appeal to buyers' self-image. All automobile brands, such as Mercedes, Ford, Jaguar, and BMW, have distinct and established personalities. Nevertheless, it is possible to change a brand's perceived personality with a sustained rebranding exercise. One brand that has managed to do this is Volvo, which has successfully translated its functional values into overcoming its image issues.

Volvo entered the US market in 1956 to a less-than-rousing reception. The model it chose to launch had a style more reminiscent of the austere 1940s than the more forward-looking and youth-obsessed 1950s.

The company soon overcame this by developing a strategy around its cars' resilience. The concept was: these are the cars built tough enough for the severe Scandinavian weather and road conditions.

Out of this evolved the familiar but realistic claim that Volvos were among the safest vehicles to drive. Over the following couple of decades, this was reinforced by the fact that the Volvo 144 and the luxury model 164 met all proposed US safety standards of the 1970s before they were even announced.

In 1982, Volvo introduced the 760, the first of the 700 series that would become a favorite family automobile of the "yuppie" (young, upwardly mobile) set in the 1980s. In 1985, Volvo became the best-selling European import.

63

USING FUNCTIONAL CAPABILITIES (CONT.)

Does exactly what it says on the tin.

1 The UK-based woodcare company Ronseal has taken functional capability advertising to its logical conclusion. Their TV ads, through straightforward messages, create trust in the product.

2 Furniture retailer IKEA has managed to move from being a functional brand to being a "passion" purchase, backed up by clean branding design that mimics the values of its furniture.

Recently Volvo has taken its positioning a step further by finally having the confidence to move closer to lifestyle branding, while retaining its core values of safety and reliability. A clever example of this was its "Safe Sex" campaign (it's safe to have sex in a Volvo).

Another Scandinavian success story continues to be IKEA. The "flat pack" furniture retailer started out as a purely functional brand, but has since become a household name synonymous with a simple, "Modernist-lite" lifestyle.

Swedish design capabilities were always renowned, but not popularly accepted until IKEA made them a household name. What most appeals to customers about the brand is its endless lines of minimal, often inexpensive products that seem to suggest a designer, European lifestyle. That and the fact that they are intended to be easy to assemble and use.

IKEA made intelligent use of people's perceptions by branding itself as a way to "chuck out the chintz." In the late 1990s, in particular, this appealed to young couples, singles, and gay men who perhaps wanted to

disassociate themselves from their parents' taste. This was especially true at a time when they were being bombarded by images of sleek, minimalist interiors full of wood, glass, steel, and leather.

Industries where purchasing decisions are based on quality and uniqueness often focus on the functional capability of the brand. One category where this is paramount is high-tech manufacturing. Brand names in these industries act more as a reference point, where product reputations and brand designs arise from the underlying strengths of the business.

The reputation of 3M, for example, is based on its constant drive to innovate and create practical, unique, and ingenious products. The 3M brand today has a clean, crisp, and simple logo, which was developed as far back as 1977. However, it was Siegelgale, a global branding consultancy, that came up with the idea of using 3M as the umbrella identity. Before this the company used a wide variety of logos and names on all its advertising and products, without the benefit of associating them with a single brand, and a single set of brand values.

2

3
The 3M brand now has a clean, crisp, and simple logo that works well across all the different categories in which they operate.

3

BRAND IS WHERE THE HEART IS

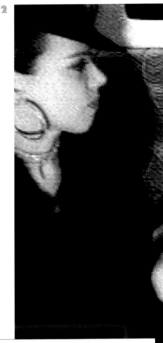

According to Marc Gobéi, in his book *Emotional Branding*, "The biggest misconception in branding strategies is the belief that branding is about market share, when it is really always about mindshare and emotions share."

Madonna's value as a brand is massive. Every time a Madonna CD is released there is an expectation that is associated not only with the music, but also with the look and feel of the CD, the accompanying videos and merchandise, the live performances, and the new ways in which the artist has found to present herself. Madonna is a massive global industry.

Like David Bowie before her, Madonna discovered the power of reinvention, and other industries from fashion, hair, and beauty products to film and even automobiles benefit from her fleeting association with a look, a culture, or a designer.

At the heart of the Madonna brand is a strong, independent woman with a commitment to excellence, and a flirtation with the cutting edge, filtered for a mainstream audience. That she has adopted the guise of other strong female figures benefits her by association, while putting her in their tradition. However, this is one brand that is focused on market share by winning hearts, minds, and wallets.

Designing the right look and feel for brands like these can be a daunting task. This is especially true when their focus on the cutting edge entails a swift and massive turnover of styles, associations, images, and typography. The brand is simply "Madonna," but unlike that other "big M,"

2
More than just a singer-songwriter and actress, Madonna has cleverly orchestrated her career so that "Madonna" is as much a brand as a name.

4
Like Madonna, David Bowie has exploited his fame (and fortune) to move into the Internet, art, and even an own-name credit card.

66

THERE'S JAGUAR AND THERE'S TRAFFIC.

XJ SERIES

1
The Jaguar website has achieved the difficult objective of reflecting their cars' personalities in a very different medium. The site says quality and craftsmanship, and the typeface and motif are aspirational.

3
New Labour has two versions of its logo. The rose and the red square have clear usage guidelines.

3

new **Labour**
new **Britain**

DAVID BOWIE · HEATHEN

67

4

McDonald's, the brand represents a set of ideas, which can be filtered through all manner of visual styles while retaining its power. If the brand runs dry, simply reinvent it.

Brand names of this type live or die on their close connections with consumers. They are fundamentally about beliefs and causes, which means staying close to their constituents' hearts. This kind of presence is nurtured by sports brands, such as football teams and basketball teams. But because they are based on belief and on building communities of support, they are harder to change and manage.

A new logo or perceived personality is potentially threatening to "heartfelt" brands, unless their appeal is built on reinvention. Because people associate themselves personally and deeply with these brands— they become a part of who they are—any change that

tampers with the brand could weaken it and ripple out among its constituents.

This applies in a different way to charities, pressure groups, and political parties, where a change of design has often been used to signal a more fundamental change of policy.

The Labour Party in the UK went through a prolonged low in the 1980s and early 1990s during its years of opposition to the Conservatives. Taking a leaf from the Democrats' book, the party signaled a change of emphasis and policy through the sustained use of new communications channels. A new logo translated the party's traditional association with the 'workers' red flag into a red rose, which they hoped would smell sweeter when planted in the center ground.

BRAND-BUYING DECISIONS

For brands whose core proposition is specialist knowledge or expertise, the best way to position them, according to author Alan Mitchell, is as "intellectual property" brands.

The industries where such branding is most appropriate are professional services, law firms, high-end information technology companies, and innovation-led packaged goods specialists.

In these cases, most of the brands are generated from the names of the organizations' founders, or are based on purely rational, rather than emotional, concepts. Examples include Ernst & Young (now Cap Gemini Ernst & Young), PricewaterhouseCoopers, J. Walter Thompson, Michael Page, Hewlett-Packard, Siebel, and McCann-Erickson.

A notable exception is management consultancy Accenture, formerly Andersen Consulting. The rebranding ("an accent on the future") took place after a complex and vicious court battle with its then sibling, accountancy giant Arthur Andersen.

But in the light of (Arthur) Andersen's subsequent disgrace and breakup in the wake of the Enron scandal, Accenture's decision to cut off all associations with the once-proud and equitable name seems remarkably prescient.

The name and logo, once mocked, have passed into the public consciousness. The design retains the proud "A" of Andersen, but its "accent on the future" (over-literally depicted in the logo) arguably protected the business from its unfortunate associations.

So, it seems that a few billions of dollars spent on litigation, strategizing, repositioning, and rebranding can pay dividends. An example of a business taking its own medicine? If nothing else, that too is a good branding exercise!

Investment bank Charles Schwab engaged Landor, a global consultancy, to identify the brand's core attributes. The company used the consultancy to develop a new wordmark (the typographical style of the company name), plus a new set of visuals, and a brand "voice." Schwab's new identity is defined as "strong, elegant, and sophisticated."

The new wordmark brings together the personal and professional aspects of the business. In design terms, it pairs a refined, cursive, and elegant "Charles" with a bold, all-capital, and functional "Schwab." The new visual vocabulary, photography style, and brand voice help to ensure recognition across a wide range of media and people.

Used together, these separate and distinct typographic elements deliver the message that Schwab offers personalized investment advice, reaffirming the confidence of existing customers and attracting new, affluent investors.

1 | 2

HSBC and PWC have both managed to create powerful brands in their categories without changing the original names globally.

HSBC

PRICEWATERHOUSE COOPERS

1

2

3 | 4

For brands such as Cap Gemini Ernst & Young their key strength lies in their people and their ability to deliver "from thought to finish." The typography is serious and professional, the colors are subtle but not boring, and they are applied universally across presentations, reports, and company information.

69

5

Although the McCann-Erickson logo bears no relation to the company's name, its message conveys the company's ethos.

5

DESIGNING A COUNTRY

One of the hardest areas to apply design to has always been that of "branding" countries for the tourist market. This is not only because it is an emotive, complex, and often controversial exercise (one that could be accused of pandering to clichéd ideas of national identity), but also because so much information is "given" and unshakable.

Within a country itself, branding exercises are often short term and politically expedient, and soon run out of steam with populations who want a return to real issues. This was certainly the case with New Labour's "Cool Britannia" exercise (its attempt to reposition Britain away from its conservative image as a land of heritage, warm beer, and cricket). But externally, exercises like these do filter through into the public consciousness.

In his landmark study on national identity, A.D. Smith in 1991 outlined the basic features of national identity as:

- An historic territory or homeland
- Common myths and historical memories
- A common mass public culture
- Common legal rights and duties for all members
- A common economy with territorial mobility for its members.

Obviously, national identity manifests itself in different and challenging ways. One person's "national identity" is another person's stereotype. This presents a uniquely difficult problem to designers who are trying to create "single" national identities for tourist boards and offices, or a design that symbolizes a complex set of values, associations—and attractions.

What might excite a German tourist to visit America, for example, might be very different from what might motivate a Japanese, an Irish, or an Italian one.

Every country has its overfamiliar symbols, which designers often resort to because they're "safe." Say

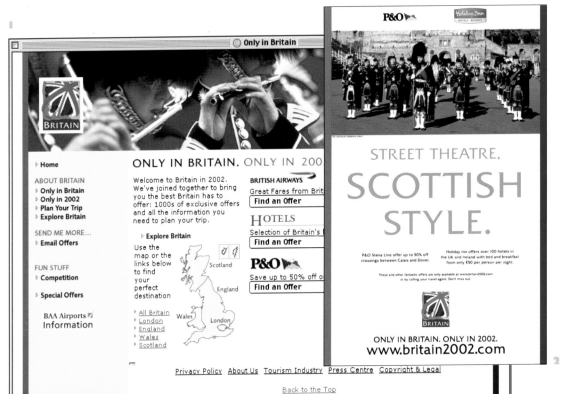

1 | 2 | 3 | 4 | 5
Britain has successfully created a strong image of providing tourists with culture, nature, fun, excitement, and romance. The "visit Britain" site has also managed to link this image to other sites for Scotland and Wales.

"England," and many tourists might think of pageantry, Big Ben, and the Tower of London. Say "Italy," and it's the Colosseum, St. Peter's, and fine works of art. Say "Holland," and it might be tulips, Rembrandt, and canals. Say "France," and it's food, the Eiffel tower, and the Riviera.

Each of the 50 American states has a similar, overarching promise: "the Sunshine State" (Florida); "the Last Frontier" (Alaska); "the Water Wonderland" (Michigan); and "the Natural State," "the Big State," or "the Lone Star" (Texas).

But all these reach for obvious symbols that have changed little in a century or more. For other groups of tourists, saying "England" might lead them to think of nightclubs, the Notting Hill Carnival, and the Glastonbury festival. Saying "Holland" might remind them of the exotic delights of Amsterdam nightlife. Saying "Italy" might bring to mind the Milan catwalks,

café culture, and Piaggio scooters. And saying "France" might make them think of high-tech parks, modern architecture, and high-speed trains.

Which would you choose? But which is right for a global, multicultural tourist industry? Designers have to make choices like these every day, and "safe" choices are not always the ones with the greatest contemporary attraction. However, contemporary choices could alienate the majority of tourists.

Some countries have managed to develop brands based almost exclusively on products that have a contemporary reputation. For example, Sweden (as we have discussed) has carved a niche based on strong design. Playsam toys, the original Saab car, Absolut Vodka, Volvo, and IKEA have all helped position the country as a center of Scandinavian excellence.

RELATIONAL BRANDS

The brand/customer relationship, if properly maintained, can be a major strength. A bond of trust between a brand and its customers can create greater brand equity, differentiating the company from the competition.

Strong brand equity allows companies to retain customers, service their needs more effectively, and increase profits. However, how can one create such a unique and close relationship with a brand that the customer's purchase becomes an "autopilot" decision?

The most important way is by demonstrating an exceptional understanding of customers' individual requirements, and reflecting this in the "look and feel" of the brand design.

Many dot.com enterprises have given new meaning to the word "personalization." Many use "cookie" technology, which allows a website to recognize an individual customer when they visit. The website can then load their personal profile and purchase record.

Dot.coms like Amazon have designed brands that focus on understanding customer habits and purchasing patterns in such a way that the customer can walk away with a pleasant experience.

But personalization involves a lot more than greeting you with your own name when you visit the site from your own computer, or log on from another with a password. It requires a brand to demonstrate an understanding of your current and future requirements.

This type of service will become increasingly prevalent with the advent of new generations of mobile services that recognize users' locations. In the near future, designers will be able to create truly personal brands that interact with customers on the move, depending on where they are and what they are doing.

The financial services sector is particularly keen on personalized services, because they create a unique experience that makes customers feel they are individually valued. MBNA has taken personalization to the next level by linking it with what is known as "affinity marketing."

The company links credit cards with various organizations—whether it is the customer's favorite charity, sports club, or university. In this way, MBNA gives customers a personalized card that creates cross-benefits between the customer, their chosen organization, and, of course, MBNA.

Another new entrant in this field is Accucard, which personalizes its cards with color schemes chosen by the customer, and also reflects that chosen personality in all its correspondence with them.

2

3

Accucard
Created for you

1 | 2 | 3 | 4 | 5
Accucard provides its cardholders with complete personalization—from colors and design to flexible financial features and benefits. The idea is that each customer can tailor the card for his or her own use, thereby taking away a reason to switch cards.

73

4

5

74

COMING TO LIFE

Once a brand and its mission, vision, and values are in place, along with a unique brand identity and a positioning that is right for the time, then the brand is ready to be implemented.

This implementation needs to be managed across all the appropriate channels so that it reaches the audience for which it is intended. Each channel, as we have explored, has a unique delivery mechanism. Brand identities need to be translated for each of these touchpoints in the most relevant and effective way. This is a challenge to designers.

Broadly speaking, there are now two main types of media: "push" and "pull." Broadcast media, including radio and (noninteractive) television, are traditionally considered "push," in that they send out programmed content that people can choose to consume or not. Either way, they cannot interact with push media. Although print media, such as periodicals and newspapers, differ greatly from radio and TV, they too are considered to fit the "push" model in principle.

Print, however, is different in that it is a medium bound by space, while traditional broadcast media are transient and bound by time, and characterized by sound and moving visuals.

Interactive media, such as the World Wide Web, conform to the "pull" model, in that consumers actively seek specific information and "pull" it from whichever sources provide it in the most authoritative, accessible, and visually attractive manner. Personalization is the logical extension of this, while broadcast, by definition, is broad and impersonal.

All of this throws down the gauntlet to brand designers. These issues become even more critical in the case of space-deficient platforms, such as cellphones, where the luxuries of video, a rich sound environment,

76

1

2

3

1 | 2 | 3
Most websites these days use standard typefaces, due to the limitations imposed by the user's computer, which may be a PC or a Mac, and by the differences between browsers, such as Explorer, Netscape, and Opera. The three sites here would have minimal branding elements once the logos are removed.

4 | 5

Some sites deliver not just the brand, but also the personality of the brand, including sites like Absolut.com.

and lush, colorful, moving graphics are promised but remain something of a bandwidth pipedream for now.

Wherever attempts have been made to merge push and pull media—such as in the case of video or TV on demand, interactive TV, fully functional digital TV, and "TV on your PC"—the level of demand has so far failed to sustain the businesses offering the services.

That situation may change in both a technological and a human generation, but at present such technologies have a tendency to offer an inferior experience at a superior price.

5

LOOK AND FEEL—PRODUCTS VS. SERVICES

In the branding world, one of the most commonly used phrases is "visual identity." This includes a brand's logo, and packaging. Packaging is an enduring expression of any brand. It has a central, strategic role to play. Expressing personality through packaging is also the most powerful way to build in "brand protection" at the design stage.

But visual identities are not just important for products on shelves competing for consumers' attention; they're vital for service brands as well. The look, feel, and layout of a bank or supermarket are just as important a way of packaging a brand as a box of soap powder is.

The principle extends to other types of service industries. JetBlue, a new US airline, has been called a "laboratory experiment in contemporary branding." JetBlue is not just an airline focusing on travel; it's about creating a "top of the class" experience, says the company.

JetBlue aims to offer economical fares, plus stylish interiors with leather seats and 24 TV channels. The flight attendants' chic, blue uniforms and the unique design of the terminal gates all wear the brand's badge of intended exclusivity.

Another example of the "look and feel" impact of design is the Evian waterdrop shape for the company's "millennium bottle." The bottle is an intelligent piece of design: eye-catching, modern, iconic, and a hint of the sensory experience of what's inside.

But perhaps the most successful recent example of using visual identity as a means of creating a powerful image of innovation is the UK vacuum cleaner and washing machine giant, Dyson. Entering a difficult and saturated market and toppling a world leader is no easy task. The key to Dyson's success has been the company's focus on both iconic, modular designs and on creating products that live up to what the visual identity promises.

78

1

2

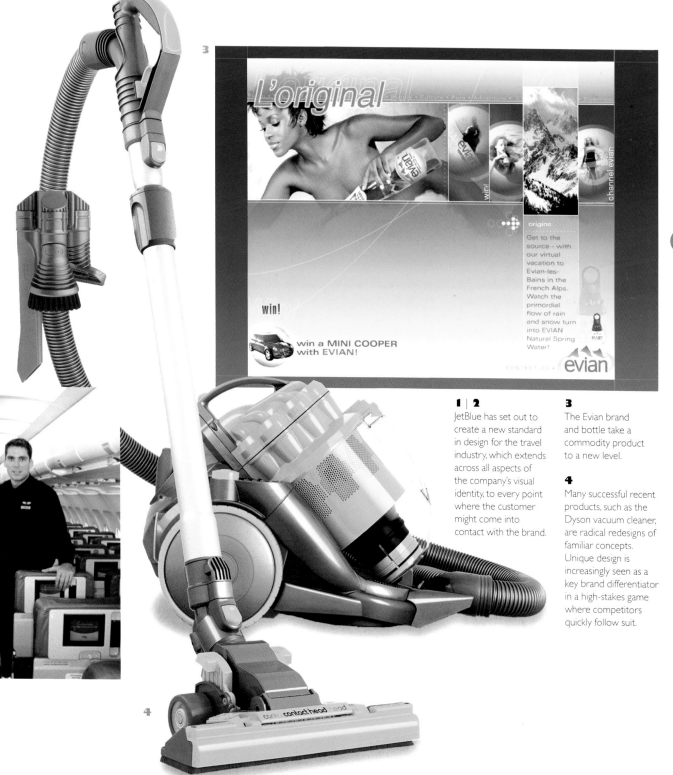

1 | 2

JetBlue has set out to create a new standard in design for the travel industry, which extends across all aspects of the company's visual identity, to every point where the customer might come into contact with the brand.

3

The Evian brand and bottle take a commodity product to a new level.

4

Many successful recent products, such as the Dyson vacuum cleaner, are radical redesigns of familiar concepts. Unique design is increasingly seen as a key brand differentiator in a high-stakes game where competitors quickly follow suit.

POWER OF THE WRITTEN WORD

The two most powerful creative tools for any brand are art (all the visual elements) and copy (the words). In most traditional media, such as newspapers and periodicals, power lies with the visuals. These are what really create the initial impact. Advertisements that convey a strong visual image and utilize few words attract much greater attention than ones that rely heavily on words to get across the message.

However, there are times when copy is crucial to a brand. First, if the message is complex. Second, if the brand is from, say, the high-tech world or another market where information can inspire purchase. Third, when the message is abstract. And finally, where slogans are instrumental in locking key messages into consumers' minds.

But to work successfully copy has to be designed correctly. Poor information design can counteract even the most well-thought-out branding campaign, and put consumers off for life. People have a tendency to speed-read advertisements. Any information that is difficult to navigate will be lost in the split second that the decision to read or bypass takes.

Some key things to keep in mind when writing advertising copy are:
• Be specific and to the point.
• Have a focus and deliver simple messages.
• Be original.
• Appear friendly and approachable, unless creating an attractive enigma is central to the brand's positioning.
• Personally address the target customer.

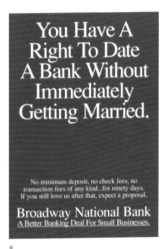

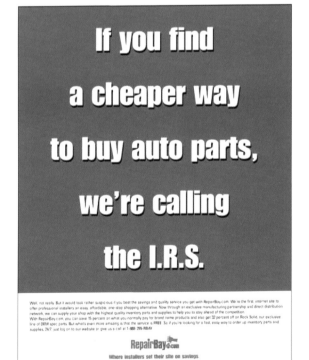

1 | 2 | 3
Copy should not only be original and engaging, but needs to be designed correctly to make the message travel a long way in people's minds.

Get bugs in your teeth.

You know who you are. What you want. Pure power. Performance without compromise. An open road. Start right here, with the **BMW R1100 R.** Come take a test-ride.

The Ultimate Riding Machine®

DEALER NAME, ADDRESS, PHONE NUMBER

©1997 BMW of North America, Inc.

4

100% Fat Free.

With this much character, you need nothing more. The **BMW R 850 R** boasts a rare combination of tradition and technology: Classic styling. Higher performance. See what counts in the real world. See us for a test-ride.

The Ultimate Riding Machine®

DEALER NAME, ADDRESS, PHONE NUMBER

©1997 BMW of North America, Inc.

5

Twist, shout and scream.

This is why they made scenic routes. The **BMW R 1100 RS.** Sport touring made aggressive, yet comfortable. Lean through the twisties with higher confidence. Relax through postcard scenes for hours. See us, for a test-ride with a view.

The Ultimate Riding Machine®

DEALER NAME, ADDRESS, PHONE NUMBER

©1997 BMW of North America, Inc.

6

Why eggs want to be laid.

WE WANT **Wall's** EST. 1786

7

WILLING TO LOSE YOUR SHIRT TO STAY IN BUSINESS?

CarCareCenter®

Not just parts. Parts Plus.

8

4 | 5 | 6
A combination of pithy, amusing copy and a powerful visual can have a strong impact on the target audience.

7 | 8 | 9
Strong copy and headlines work for most categories and products, be it food, automobiles, or soft toys.

22ND SENSORY FASHION

As we have explored, design is by far the most powerful expression of a brand. It can bring ideas to life and create a strong link between manufacturer, seller, and buyer. The Jaguar X series, Prada bags, the Mini, and bottles of Absolut are all examples of products that demonstrate how design creates emotions, sensory experiences... and sales.

Some brands, however, take the idea to extremes to create an overarching brand experience that defines everything else they do.

Designing sensory experiences creates a rapport with some customers. Sensory experiences are instant, potent, and capable of influencing buying decisions in both the long and short term. This is why "traditional" retail in many major urban centers is viewed by some as an outmoded activity.

In its place is the "art of shopping," which is less about purchasing and more about creating all-embracing experiences of a brand—experiences that people talk about. They prosper every time someone says, "Have you been to Brand X City?"

Niketown in London and New York is a good example of a "self-perpetuating" brand experience, where word of mouth among peer groups creates the impetus to visit. In many ways, the notion of building an entire world to reflect a brand's values originated with Disney, of course. Other companies want that kind of presence, and the idea is often now adapted to purely retail environments.

The New York Niketown store covers almost 70,000 square feet, has five floors, and was designed by Nike Design and Boora architects to be a "shrine" to the brand. The shining glass and steel structure within a traditional-looking brick shell certainly creates an impression that customers remember for a long time.

Buying trainers or sportswear from Niketown, or visiting Warner Village for films, food, and games, is designed to be like moving into a neighborhood where

you are one of the right crowd, and you can meet other people just like you who share the brand's values.

In the case of Niketown and Disneyland/Disney World, scarcity is vital. The brand might be ubiquitous, global, and familiar to all, but the "all in" experience is available in only a small number of places.

These are designed to be the "apotheosis" of a brand, its ultimate statement, so that if the brand defines the customer in some way, the customer will travel to reach the purest expression of it. Even if they never visit, most will be aware of its existence. This type of aspirational branding becomes self-perpetuating. It also demands that the company gets it right, which means colossal expense.

To succeed, brands that create this type of experience have to be certain that there are sufficient numbers of customers dedicated enough to become part of a community, while providing a service that "passers by" might want from time to time in a heavily populated city.

1
Habitat has created a website that truly reflects the in-store experience.

2
Niketown is an example of creating a brand experience in the true sense of the word.

3
Sears has created a public image of itself as a family store, both in the merchandise it carries and in intangible elements such as warmth, comfort, friendliness, honesty, and even selflessness.

But in order to keep the momentum going, all-in "experience" brands have to stay ahead to survive, and keep offering something new, such as constantly evolving product lines where older models are swiftly deleted.

"Brand X City" could quickly become a ghost town if the brand strayed from its objectives, or there was a sudden shift in fashion away from a constant and expensive cycle of fashionable upgrades. The faster a brand moves, the faster it has to keep moving.

Nevertheless, many of these experienced brands have survived rollercoasters of good and bad publicity; such has been the power of the brand for its constituency.

Experience designing is found in subtler forms in many less obviously branded retail ventures. For example, the Rainforest Café pumps fresh-flower extracts into its retail sections, and Jordan furniture stores in Massachusetts use scents such as bubble gum in the children's section, and pine in the country style section.

BROADCAST MEDIA

One of the most commonly used media to create brand awareness and communicate with an audience is broadcast, specifically TV and radio. TV in particular has numerous advantages over other media (with the exception of cinema advertising), including high budgets, creative potential, breadth of impact and exposure, captivity, interest, and flexibility.

The greatest advantage of TV is undoubtedly the prospect of designing a branding message for the broadest possible audience. TV commercials are increasingly used to express a mood, feeling, experience, or image that makes everyday products seem special and unique.

Most people own a TV, so the medium is ideal for products that have mass appeal. However, having such a big target to hit makes it harder to design advertising that is aimed at small sections of the overall audience. To an extent, however, this hurdle can be overcome with effective media planning.

This is achieved by reviewing the profile of viewers at certain times of the day (such as Sunday morning), or the audience profiles of specific programs, such as a drama about a group of young, upwardly mobile lawyers, for example.

Advertisers can also adjust their media strategies to take advantage of different geographical markets through local ("spot") adverts in specific market areas. Adverts can be scheduled to run repeatedly, or to take advantage of special occasions.

The advantages of radio are mainly in the lower cost, and the fact that listeners tend not to tune out whenever advertisements come on. Radio stations have more loyal listeners, and advertisers can select the station whose listeners most closely reflect their target audience.

However, radio does restrict what brand designers can convey, so they have to find a way of reflecting the brand's identity using an audio-only medium. (Digital radio does promise limited visual elements, but its potential audience is, as yet, far from proven.)

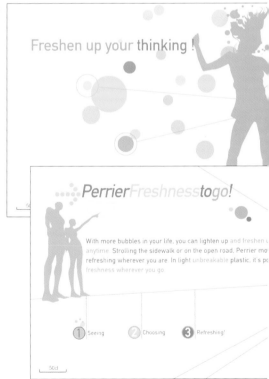

1 | 2 | 3
Perrier have translated
their values of
freshness very
successfully across
all media.

4 | 5
Even though the
execution is very
different, both Nike
and Mini have used
broadcast media to
convey the aspirational
aspect of their brands.

PRINTED MATTER—NEWSPAPERS AND PERIODICALS

Newspapers and, especially, periodicals are two of the most widely used mediums to develop brands' appeal with their audience.

Newspaper advertising is one of the few forms that is not considered to be too intrusive. But when creating a newspaper advert, the designer has to keep in mind that most newspapers are printed at very high speed on inexpensive, rough-surfaced paper called newsprint, which quickly absorbs ink on contact.

The "dot gain" of newsprint (where each tiny dot of ink expands as if on blotting paper) means that fine details are often hard to reproduce. Light typefaces are recommended for large amounts of text, as the typeface will appear heavier when printed. Fine details, however, will be lost.

Newsprint is also not the easiest medium on which to reproduce color photographs. Most papers offer some color advertising opportunities. However, the limitations of the newspaper printing process mean that the four-color plates might be out of register (not be perfectly aligned), leading to a fuzzy or confusing image. Unlike periodicals, newspapers cannot afford to maintain strict levels of print quality control.

Newspapers are usually printed in page sections that are multiples of four (in periodicals it is usually multiples of eight). Most newspapers, then, will run perhaps an eight- or sixteen-page section with full color. This may limit a color advertisement's placement options.

Periodicals have grown to cater to very different requirements and markets, from educational to informational, from business to consumer, and from entertainment to fashion, health, and lifestyle. This makes them a specialized and highly sophisticated branding medium.

86

1 | 2
Different layouts have different roles to play and have a major impact on the success of an advertisement or campaign.

3
Levis have linked their TV campaigns with the execution of print and other formats of advertising to reinforce the message to their target audience.

readers of *Maxim* or *Loaded*, are, in theory, different to the readers of *GQ* or *Attitude*. In practice, of course, this is not always the case, but it's the theory that counts.

This is because most consumer periodicals are aimed at a "fictional reader." Before launching a new periodical, editors and designers will draw up a detailed description of who this person is: how old he or she is; their income bracket; their lifestyle; where they shop; what clothes they wear; what music they listen to; what they do with their leisure time; where they live; and what they do for a living. The periodical is then aimed squarely at that reader, and he or she forms the advertising proposition that brands use to find the best match.

"Business-to-business" magazines offer a similar proposition. Many are what is known as "controlled circulation." This simply means that the periodical is only mailed out to someone who has the specific job title that the magazine is aimed at, say, chief finance officer or chief information officer. In this way, publishers can approach brands and say, "One hundred percent of our readers are chief executives. Your brand is aimed at chief executives and decision makers, so place your advertisement with us."

The reproduction quality of most periodicals is extremely high, so publishers can promise that a brand's visual identity will be faithfully reproduced. Their advertisements are also using more and more creative, attention-grabbing devices such as pop-up visuals, scent strips, gatefold covers, and even computer chips that play melodies.

One of the main advantages is magazines' selectivity and ability to target specific audiences. The readers of *Vogue* or *Elle*, for example, are in theory very different to the readers of *Woman's Own* or *Woman's World*; and the

GRAB ATTENTION IN THREE SECONDS

Direct mail and marketing are powerful tools for consumer-facing brands. There is now a host of subsets, such as relationship marketing, permission marketing, and one-to-one marketing—all of which are sophisticated ways to target and build relationships with individual consumers.

The format and layout of direct mails are the two crucial design factors that determine the success of any campaign. Of course, the research prior to the campaign, the testing of the concept and media, and the proposition itself are vital strategic elements, but it is the art direction that provides the delivery.

The key elements of the mailout are copy, images, and delivery format. The copy should be tight and unique to the brand (even if you take the brand name out, customers should still know who you are talking about). The copy should also pass the "three second test": if the customer looks quickly at the headlines and captions, will they be inspired to read the rest?

But most importantly, the copy should be, to use marketing jargon, "actionable."

Beyond this, images are what bring the copy to life, and a single, striking visual is often the best way to hook a potential customer.

The format of a direct mail determines whether or not the mail will even get opened. The envelope is vital, and half the battle is getting the customer to open it. One method companies use is preselling, by putting an enticing fact about a special offer, for example, on the envelope itself.

Interestingly, making a consumer mailout look businesslike works well, while making a business mailout look more "consumery" is also a good way of attracting attention.

Direct mail must attract attention immediately. Unsurprisingly, the word "free" features widely in such campaigns.

free Parker pen when you ask for a free quote

Call us today for a no-obligation, written quote and see how much you could save by switching your buildings and

up to £30 free Marks & Spencer vouchers

- £15 when you take out buildings insurance
- £15 when you take out home contents insurance

When you take out home insurance with us, you could have up to £30 worth of Marks & Spencer vouchers to spend on whatever you want. £15 with your buildings insurance and £15 with your contents cover. To find out how much you could save, call us today on **0800 092 1003** or buy online at www.insurance.co.uk

Lloyds TSB

Insurance

2 | 3 | 4
These are examples of some very effective campaigns done by major brands: AOL, the British bank Lloyds TSB, and Ford.

4

 89

BRAND ON THE RUN

Developing wireless applications for mobile devices (such as cellphones and PDAs) presents an exceptional set of challenges. Some of the unique problems faced by designers creating applications and user interfaces for branding strategies in the wireless environment are:

• **Limited bandwidth**: A wireless device typically has much less bandwidth available for transmitting and receiving data than a wired device. Third-generation (3G) mobile networks promise "broadband" connectivity.

• **Intermittent connection**: The connection to a wireless device is often unreliable. A persistent point-to-point connection is difficult.

• **Limited memory on client device**: Once again, because of the mobile nature of wireless devices and their need to remain small, memory space is currently limited. Memory is also limited by the available power source (batteries) on the device.

• **Limited processing power**: Because of the size of the devices and the battery life, processing information on the device is very expensive. Very few operations should be performed on the device and they should only be performed where there is strong justification for them.

• **Limited user interface**: A usable keyboard and/or a mouse are often not available for a wireless or small mobile device. The display is almost always small as well. This makes viewing and data entry more difficult.

Downloading data from the Internet on an information appliance, therefore, is slow, unstable, and expensive. Most people are not interested in reading long articles on their digital assistants, but they would, however, like to gain access to data such as stock quotes, news headlines, travel arrangements, online banking, gambling opportunities, weather reports, and simple location-based services.

Designing information for delivery on such a device starts with creating content that will be useful, accessible, swift to deliver, and easy to navigate. Most devices today don't have a full keyboard option and require simple button functions.

Desktop computers have made color an indispensable part of the user interface. On a PDA screen, with smaller icons and more potential for clutter, color could be just as useful. But that doesn't mean that more color is better. Among usability experts, the mantra regarding color is the familiar "less is more."

1
Brands like Virgin have proven that the cellphone industry is just as brand driven as other consumer products.

2
Not many brands have satisfactorily moved into wireless media, but a few have done it successfully. Most devices cannot support cascading style sheets and have screens with limited capability. The simpler the interface, the better.

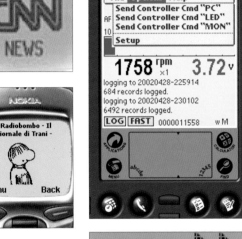

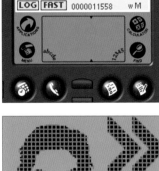

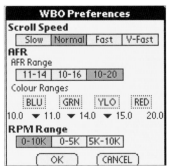

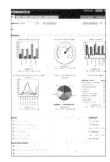

BILLBOARDS AND CITY LIGHTS

Messages posted in public areas can give a branding message real impact, and create spin-off publicity. Posters and billboards remain an important form of advertising, and feature some iconic examples of design and photography.

The key to an effective billboard campaign is a single, striking visual with minimal copy. It should be built on a strong creative concept that communicates its message quickly, attracts attention, and is easy to remember.

A dominant headline can act as a product signal. A short, catchy phrase works best, especially if it is a play on words or a twist on a common phrase.

1

2

It's important to remember that billboards need to work from a distance, and be able to attract attention from a distance as well, especially if placed near fast-moving traffic. All outdoor campaigns are likely to be seen at all times of the day and night, and under all kinds of driving and lighting conditions.

However, billboards are not the only type of outdoor advertising: there is also street furniture (such as on street lights, benches, or on "adshells" at bus shelters), "transit" advertising (on buses, vans, cabs, and so on), and "alternative" campaigns, such as ones using inflatables, or which take over a familiar landmark or construction site.

3

 Billboards obviously need to work from a distance, but they also need to grab attention quickly, otherwise the message will be lost on often fast-moving traffic.

4

1 | 2 | 3

Key images, colors, and visuals all play a very important role in making a billboard effective, especially in crowded spaces.

4 | 5 | 6

A single striking image together with short, punchy copy is the key to a successful transit advertisement.

3

5

95

4

6

The most important design considerations for outdoor advertising are:

• **Graphics**: The image should be eye-catching and attractive, from any distance.

• **Colors**: Use bold, bright colors. Maximum impact is created by contrasting two colors, dark versus light. Black-and-white photography works well for this reason.

• **Subject and background**: Ensure that the relationship between foreground and background is clearly defined. The background should never compete with the subject.

• **Typography**: It is best to use simple, clean, uncluttered type that is easy to read at a distance, especially by people in motion.

• **Lighting**: You can create compelling visuals on illuminated billboards against a night sky, particularly on those that change, rotate, or contain neon.

• **Shape**: For visual impact create the illusion of three-dimensional effects by playing with horizons, vanishing lines, and dimensional boxes.

The rules for transit advertising are slightly different. Transit advertising is targeted at the millions of people who use commercial transportation such as buses, cabs, commuter trains, metros, trams, elevators, trolleys, and airplanes. In many cases, such as when ads appear on metro platforms or on trains, the campaign can be more text-heavy, as potential customers have more time to read. But a single, striking image is still the incentive for people to read the advertiser's message in the first place.

SALES PROMOTIONS

Sales promotions are directed at the real end-users of a product. The purpose is to presell a concept or an idea to consumers, so that when they go to a store they look for the product (as opposed to the product having to "shout" from crowded shelves to attract attention).

The main types of sales promotions are:
• Samples, where the customer can experience, taste, smell, touch, or hear the product in a small, single-use format, such as a free sachet of shampoo, a free cup of a new drink, or a sample bottle of scent.
• Discounts to encourage the purchase of a new or competitive product. This is sometimes risky, as it creates both a precedent and the idea that the product has to be made less expensive to sell.
• A "20 percent extra free" campaign, where customers get more for the same price.
• Coupons that can be part of a collectable series, leading to a gift.
• Sweepstakes and competitions.

Sample promotions create a unique opportunity to encapsulate a brand's visual identity and design ethos, as they are mini versions of the product itself, backed by a marketing push. In effect, they allow customers to "test drive" a product. This works well for fast-moving consumer goods (fmcg) and cosmetics in particular.

When sample promotions are presented at in-store kiosks, or at kiosks in public places such as railway stations or airports, brands can create a real sense of excitement around their product. Even if potential customers do not stop and take a sample, the presence of dozens of people milling around a kiosk is often as good an advertisement as the product itself. People feel they are missing out if they don't join the throng.

Coupons encourage loyalty toward products, even if customers have yet to try the goods. Brand owners sometimes encourage customers to buy a certain number of products before they receive a promised benefit, such as a gift, a free quantity of the product, or another product from the same manufacturer (which may be the hidden purpose of the campaign).

96

Instead of lowering prices (which creates a precedent), many brands prefer to give away extra product. This avoids creating the impression that their product can be sold more cheaply. This is a design opportunity to "amend" the brand.

11

Consumers love the idea of winning a car or holiday when purchasing a low-value item.

IF HOMER CAN, WHY CAN'T I?

A large number of companies are increasingly using celebrity associations to create a specific personality type for their brand, or to adopt a celebrity's personality by association. Many brands only come to life when they find the appropriate face to front them. Sports personalities in particular bring with them associations of health, youth, vitality, clean living, individual achievement, and—with the likes of the golfer Tiger Woods, the tennis player Anna Kournikova, and the UK soccer star David Beckham— good looks and personal style.

When they find the right face or personality, some brands seize the opportunity to reinvent their visual identities for a new age.

Watch brand Tag Heuer has launched several global advertising campaigns using sports personalities. It has moved away from its former image of being rugged, cold, machinelike, and technically efficient to being seen as a brand that is warm and human, yet still technically superb.

By using stylish sports personalities, such as former tennis superstar Boris Becker, such brands can align themselves with the abstract, aspirational concepts associated with sporting excellence. Ideas such as using mental toughness and self-control to overcome adversity or succeed appeal to people who see themselves as winners, or who would like to be.

Movie or soap actors such as Brad Pitt, Jennifer Anniston, and dozens of others sometimes lend their faces to advertising campaigns, particularly away from their home territories where advertising is less likely to damage their core appeal. Singers and pop stars are also popular. In 2002, for example, Coca-Cola and Pepsi signed up Christina Aguilera and Britney Spears, respectively, to front TV campaigns.

This, though, is just the tip of the iceberg of celebrity endorsement: drinks companies and other brands frequently sponsor live music events and other big shows.

98

1
Coca-Cola uses Christina Aguilera to front a TV campaign in the hope that it will help to ingratiate the soft drink to a younger audience.

2
In 2000, Venus Williams became one of the sports personalities to support Reebok. Her unique style appeals to young people. Her contract was used as a launch pad for a campaign called "Defy Convention."

2

3

99

400 patents each year, making your beauty dreams reality.
BECAUSE **YOU'RE WORTH IT.**

L'ORÉAL
PARiS

4

5

CONTROLLING A WWW IDENTITY

When companies first started using the Internet it was mainly to disseminate information, usually in the form of dull, unattractive-looking text. At best, most sites were online catalogs that people could browse and pull information from.

Now websites have become colorful, animated, and interactive sensory experiences that can be personalized and individualized to reflect the customer's individual choices, preferences, interests, and needs.

So what makes a site successful? Broadly speaking, the objectives of a website can be grouped into nine categories:

- Information distribution
- Awareness
- Gathering information about customer choices, preferences, and buying habits
- Creating and sustaining a brand image and reputation
- Encouraging the trial of new products and services
- Improving customer service and the brand's relationship with its community of users
- Selling products and services
- Offering unique "value-added" services—such as Nike's "design your own trainers online" offering
- Migrating customers toward a low-cost channel for one-to-one business.

One source of revenue for many companies continues to be online advertising, although few brands have built a sustainable business model or revenue stream from their Internet presence. Indeed, most companies find that the Web works best as a low-cost channel through which to build customer relationships and create a community of individual users.

It is also a uniquely successful means of gathering data about customers' choices and preferences, and of designing a personalized experience for them (hence the growth of "My Brand X" portals that the user has the ability to customize).

Since the days of banner adverts and "skyscrapers" (vertical banners), most online advertisers have become far more creative in the design of their branding presences. Interstitials, pop-up windows, and other advert styles are increasingly commonplace.

The key challenge for brands that advertise online is to ensure that the brand values are delivered correctly, and that the objective of the advertising is clear. If the advertising is tactical, then the design should encourage click-throughs (to the brand's own site) and a maximum response rate. If, on the other hand, the aim is strategic (i.e., brand building), then the message should be both clear and compelling in its design.

Many brands are also finding that the Web provides an unusual opportunity to extend the brand into new areas, such as online film or video competitions, and other types of creative Web ventures that sell neither products nor services, but encourage customers to

102

1 | 2
Banner advertising is still the most popular form of advertising on the Web, but the formats have developed and grown from buttons to banners, to skyscrapers and rich media banners.

3
The Gap shopping website reflects the experience of shopping in one of Gap's stores. The typography is clean and uncluttered, the design is modern yet accessible, and the range of clothes available is mixed and varied.

participate in activities that extend the brand's ethos, values, and visual identity. Games, gambling, chatrooms, and a host of other community activities can be designed to make people feel part of what the brand stands for.

And because technology is advancing so quickly, broadband Web access, larger memory capacities, and faster processors mean that many websites can now successfully combine elements and design styles from different media, such as print, sound, music, video, animation, and games. The challenge for designers here is easy navigation, and balancing eye-catching visuals, animation, graphics, video, and sound with swift download times that don't frustrate the visitor.

Graphics should be eye-catching, but not confusing, without demanding too much download time. Typography should be simple, but unique. Some typographical elements will need to be saved as graphics files in order to display on the customer's computer. As a rule of thumb, designers should use few typefaces, and avoid clashing colors, or colors that are difficult to read against the background. Finally, designers should bear in mind that different computing platforms and browsers mean that typefaces will not always display correctly, and another typeface might be substituted.

TAKING TV TO THE NEXT STAGE

Interactive television (iTV) is one of the most recent and fascinating developments in interactive media. Historically, the television has always been a one-way communication format, where a mixed program of information, news, and entertainment has been broadcast to the widest possible audience.

However, consumers now have the ability to interact with the television in the same way they can with the Internet, while also having access to a huge variety of more "targeted" channels, offering just music, shopping, movies, and so on. These are the televisual equivalents of periodicals, in terms of having an entire schedule of programmed content aimed at a clearly defined audience.

Television can now be used for obtaining a wide variety of information, shopping, games, entertainment, and many other services. Many well-known consumer brands have managed to make the transition into interactive TV very successfully, but only because they have understood the principles of how consumers interact with the medium.

Interactive TV services in Europe exist within a "walled garden" instead of residing on the public Internet. Limited Internet access (such as to specific sites) is available through some interactive services, as it is through cable and satellite.

Under such circumstances, a broadcaster has control over both the overall environment and the consumer's experience. A broadcaster's electronic programming guide (EPG), with links from video advertisements, directs users to interactive services.

Technically, interactive services function differently from the way Web access on a PC does. While set-top boxes include modems for two-way communication, most of the interactivity occurs locally—within the set-top box, rather than over a completely open connection to the Internet.

Interactivity via TV falls into the following categories:

• **One-way**: Teletext, which broadcasts data along with normal video programming and the EPG, does not use a return path. The data is broadcast continuously.

• **Local**: Simple games and enhanced content are stored locally in the set-top box. Broadcasters may or may not use the return path to allow viewers to request additional data.

• **Two-way**: Interactive advertising, banking, and shopping all require a return path to process transactions. However, most of the interactivity remains local, which alleviates the need to open up modems for simple applications.

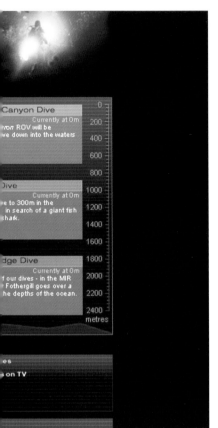

1 | 2 | 3

Navigation and ease of use will continue to remain the key issues when designing interactive TV sites. Sites that have used simple colors effectively include Abyss live, AOL TV, and many others.

• **Real-time**: Although multiplayer gaming is not yet available on interactive TV, some broadcasters plan to offer it in the near future.

Designers have to remember that navigation and simplicity are central to making a brand work successfully on interactive TV. The majority of consumers interact with iTV via a remote control, although add-on keyboards are available (but are not currently popular).

It is vital to remember that certain colors do not reproduce well on TV monitors, so brand designers will have to ensure that any brand designed for the iTV environment must fall within accepted boundaries.

ART AND GUERRILLA MARKETING

Guerrilla marketing took off during the Internet boom, with most companies running out of marketing dollars as they underestimated the task of creating brands from scratch, not to mention revenue streams.

With consumers ranking word-of-mouth as the most effective means of tempting them to visit a website, advertisers started to break through the online and offline advertising noise and generate a buzz through brand-relevant, integrated guerrilla marketing.

Guerrilla marketing, the use of unconventional methods to gain visibility, has helped many sites rise above the advertising clutter. When executed effectively, guerrilla marketing campaigns are unique, unexpected, and memorable—grabbing consumers' attention and forcing them to take notice.

Such tactics also increase the effectiveness of marketing campaigns at comparatively little cost.

Some of the techniques commonly employed are:

- **Man on the street**: Employees of the company or hired reps interact with consumers on a one-to-one basis.
- **Offline sampling**: Companies distribute branded merchandise to consumers in an effort to drive traffic to, and sales from, an online property. Offline sampling is often part of a "man on the street" campaign.
- **Alternative outdoor**: Companies place nontraditional, nonmeasurable outdoor advertisements, including wild postings—posters informally tacked up in public areas, often around construction areas in cities—in highly visible locations.
- **Viral marketing**: Consumers are given an incentive to pass along promotional messages and offers, generally through email messages, becoming, in effect, part of the company's salesforce.
- **Online buzz tactics**: Employees of the company, or hired representatives, seed newsgroups, chatrooms, or fan sites in an effort to generate a buzz online and drive traffic to specific sites.

One company that used these techniques very successfully was PetsMart.com. In an effort to better target pet owners on a personal and regional level (and put a "face" to the brand), the online retailer of pet supplies and merchandise initiated a man-on-the-street campaign as part of its guerrilla marketing program.

PetsMart.com created its campaigns through an in-house group working in conjunction with external agencies. The company's marketing department developed ideas, with one full-time employee in the group devoted to guerrilla marketing efforts.

To carry out the strategy, PetsMart.com trained what it called "brand ambassadors" in how to communicate the brand correctly and effectively. The company then dispatched its ambassadors to public dog runs and dog-related events, many of which it sponsors, in key cities.

The brand ambassadors then distributed branded tennis balls, dog biscuits, cards, flyers, t-shirts, and hats to dog owners, with the aim of putting the PetsMart.com name into each person's hand and initiating relationships

2
Companies place nontraditional, nonmeasurable outdoor ads, including wild postings, to increase alternative attention for their brands.

1
Creating a buzz online is nowadays an important aspect of building brands on the Net.

3
A large number of unsolicited advertisements and promotions are now being sent via people's fax machine numbers.

4
In the weeks prior to the release of teen pop singer Christina Aguilera's debut album, RCA Records hired a group of young online users to promote the singer on popular teen chat sites and newsgroups in an effort to create a positive buzz and drive record sales.

with potential customers. The company supplemented these initiatives with local offline marketing efforts.

PetsMart.com managed to extend its man-on-the-street campaign to include parties at pet adoption centers and dog fashion shows, which it calls "Canine Couture" events. These created goodwill throughout the local pet-owning community—often raising money for charity while simultaneously raising awareness of the brand.

The results were exceptional. The success of guerrilla marketing efforts is often difficult to measure, but PetsMart.com executives report that the site sees regional sales spikes whenever it runs its man-on-the-street events.

CREATING BRAND MEMORIES

People generally remember the first time they saw a favorite movie, or heard a song that became important to them because it coincided with a significant time in their lives. People develop deep, personal associations with this type of thing—something that some brands use as the inspiration for designing equally memorable experiences.

The periodical *Business Week* calls the trend "nostalgia marketing." Many brands rerun TV advertisements that professional, adult customers will remember from their schooldays. The aim is to recreate the feelings they had when they first saw them, and to renew their acquaintance with the brand by appealing to that nostalgia.

Other brands make knowing references to their pasts: the new Volkswagen Beetle and the new Mini are two examples of brand designs that have reinvented a "classic" for a new era. Both of these designs have their roots in the middle of the last century.

By doing so, brands can rediscover their own roots and core values, and remind themselves (and their customers) what they have achieved and where they

have come from. For example, when you visit the Coca-Cola website you can see the company proudly displaying its history. This move captures generations of customers, while the brand's principal focus can still remain on attracting the young.

The Coca-Cola site is replete with references to days gone by; a fond and nostalgic time warp. Mercedes-Benz is another brand that helps us to remember the past—its past, and ours by association.

The "Of Legends and Passion" section of Mercedes' website reveals a brand keen to associate itself with a fine tradition, and with the good memories its customers have of their own days gone by. Indeed, the company's centennial celebrations in 2001 saw it dusting off its past advertising to remind us of its history of innovation decade by decade.

Unexpected delivery is another way of building a brand memory. Consumers have become jaded enough to know what to expect from a brand experience. Giving them something new, unexpected, or "out of the box" helps create brand memory.

1

2

Home　　**National**　　**Suchen**　　**Site-Map**　　**Dialog**

Mercedes-Benz

News & Events
MB Classic
History
　Biographies
　Vehicle History
　Truck History
　Bus History
　Unimog History
　Motor Sport History
　Races and Records
　Design

The History Behind the Mercedes-Benz Brand and the Three-Pointed Star

Gottlieb Daimler and Karl Benz

The invention in the 1880s of the high-speed engine and the automobile enabled Gottlieb Daimler and Karl Benz – independently of one another – to lay the foundations for the motorization of road transport. With the help of financial backers and partners, they both invested their development projects in their own private businesses – in Mannheim, Benz founded the firm Benz & Cie. in October 1883, and Daimler-Motoren-Gesellschaft (DMG) was formed in November 1890.

In order to gain publicity and a certain distinction for their products, both companies sought a suitable trademark. To begin with, the inventors used their own names – "Benz" and "Daimler", which vouched for the origin and quality of the engines and vehicles. The trademark of Benz & Cie. remained unchanged, except that in 1909, the cog wheel symbol which had been used since 1903 was replaced with a laurel wreath surrounding the name Benz. But the turn of the century brought a completely new trade name for products from Daimler-Motoren-Gesellschaft (DMG) in Cannstatt: "Mercedes". So what is the origin of this name?

JACK DANIEL'S HEAD DISTILLER, Jimmy Bedford, has lots of folks looking over his shoulder

Since 1866, we've had only six head distillers. (Every one a Tennessee boy, starting with Mr. Jack Daniel himself.) Like those before him, Jimmy's mindful of our traditions, such as the oldtime way we smooth our whiskey through 10 feet of hard maple charcoal. He knows Jack Daniel's drinkers will judge him with every sip. So he's not about to change a thing. The five gentlemen on his wall surely must be pleased about that.

SMOOTH SIPPIN'
TENNESSEE WHISKEY

4
The heritage and history are an integral part of the advertising strategy of Jack Daniels.

5
The Coca-Cola website is full of references to days gone by.

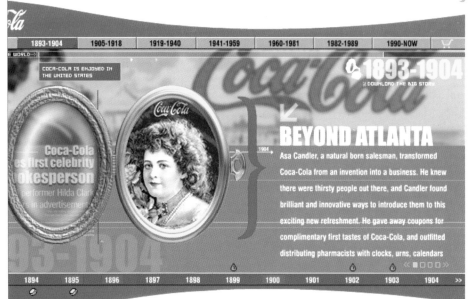

BEYOND ATLANTA

Asa Candler, a natural born salesman, transformed Coca-Cola from an invention into a business. He knew there were thirsty people out there, and Candler found brilliant and innovative ways to introduce them to this exciting new refreshment. He gave away coupons for complimentary first tastes of Coca-Cola, and outfitted distributing pharmacists with clocks, urns, calendars

109

1 | 2 | 3
Mini and Mercedes both use their heritage to reinforce the values of their brand.

6
Derived from the original painting by Francis Barraud, the contemporary HMV logo has kept its original feel while updating the image to meet today's demands.

top dog for music·video·games

TAKING BRANDS ACROSS CULTURES

Designing and managing a global brand creates many testing challenges for a brand owner. Global branding is a process whereby a brand owner can sensibly and successfully translate a product or service from one market to another.

However, the key to global branding success lies in understanding local diversity, idiosyncrasies, and usage patterns before taking a product or service across geographical boundaries.

Many brands today have built a global proposition by understanding and stressing local difference, or, conversely, by designing a deliberately multicultural and multiethnic visual identity (as in the case of, for example, United Colors of Benetton).

The investment bank Morgan Stanley's campaign "One client at a time," HSBC's advertising of local traditions, and British Airways' ill-fated, but bold, decision to display on its tail fins local artists' paintings from the territories it serves are all examples of global thinking.

Some nations are beginning to examine their own branding (as we discussed on page 70) as highly as at government level. For example, the Philippines began considering it following a seminar there by Philip Kotler about how the international community viewed the country, while New Zealand's influential *Unlimited* periodical devoted a feature to the New Zealand "national brand."

Even the US media have begun questioning the country's image in the wake of anti-American (and anti-globalization) demonstrations throughout the world. This, in some ways, is the other side of the coin of many brands' success, as companies have (rightly or wrongly) come to signify the culture of their country of origin.

Most nations want to be seen as progressive, environmentally conscious, a good place to do business, along with a host of other qualities. No national branding program will succeed if that image does not stand up to scrutiny.

110

By emphasizing unity in diversity in their campaigns, Benetton have emphasized the global nature of their business.

UNITED COLORS
OF BENETTON.

BRAND REVIVAL

It's easy to blame fragile economies when a brand starts to lose its value, but there are usually other, more fundamental considerations. Sometimes brands simply lose touch with consumers, particularly if they have dominated a market for a long time. On other occasions, though, the problem is the category itself: technology is removing some brands by making their categories obsolete.

Many companies are victims of their own success. If a company that produces dozens of successful products becomes synonymous with only one of them, then that brand becomes locked in people's minds as standing for one thing alone.

If the brand stands for an idea, such as "security" (in the case of Chubb, for example), then the company can simply keep innovating and develop new products that fit that overarching idea. But if the brand has been successfully positioned to represent a single product or product category, then the company can face problems if the category is threatened by the march of technology.

For example, successful brands such as Polaroid (which built itself up until it was synonymous with instant photography) and Kodak (which did the same with film photography) have seen the categories they represent decline due to digital photography.

Brands can lose touch both with the customer and with where the brand exists in popular culture— something that moves fast and is also fragmenting and mutating in ways it has never done before.

Simple tribal youth cultures that were once centered on music have become increasingly complex. They are spreading across the boundaries of youth and deeper

1 | 2
Some brands weaken due to a perceived lack of relevance, even if they have successfully diversified into other areas. Polaroid, for example, is identified strongly with instant photography, a category that is being undermined by inexpensive digital cameras and PCs.

FHM

OCTOBER 2002 £3.10 WWW.FHM.COM

MAKE US LAUGH, FATMAN!

Johnny Vegas, Peter Kay & Ricky Gervais star in our TV Comedy Special

PUT THE STAPLER DOWN, NORMAN!'
When geeks go bad!

YOU CRASH, YOU DIE!
We straddle the world's fastest bikes

PAULINA RUBIO!

Attention amigos! It's Mexico's hottest

SEX YOU DON'T DESERVE!

How to lie and cheat your way into her pants

100 KILLER INTERNET SITES!

'HOW ARE YOU BOOKED FOR 2040, VICAR?'
The date of your death – revealed!

3

4

3 | 4
The UK magazine *FHM* (formerly *For Him Magazine*) has created a very clear market position in a difficult and cluttered marketplace. It has stood the test of time and remained at the forefront.

113

BRAND REVIVAL (CONT.)

into adulthood, as people in their late 20s and 30s continue to go to nightclubs and music events. Meanwhile, the youth market itself is more and more obsessed with gaming and technology.

Fashions, as we all know, change quickly, and we're on a fast track. Brands that don't keep up are quickly lost. They first become inappropriate, then invisible, and then they're gone.

This is certainly true of periodical publishing, an industry that traditionally moves fast to identify new groups of readers, and designs products quickly for them. But for the same reason, periodicals can have a short shelf life. One such brand was *Mademoiselle*, a periodical that lost touch with its readers and folded. Despite a long and rich history, *Mademoiselle* was too late on feminism and working women at the time. The title got out of sync culturally.

Periodical publishing is a high-risk business when brands are misconceived, or companies believe they can read the Zeitgeist, only to find they are wrong. In

the late 1980s, UK brand Carlton, which had successfully built a stable of lifestyle and women's periodicals, poured so much capital into a new launch, *Riva*, that when it failed the company collapsed after just a few issues of the title. It saw a gap in the market that simply was not there, a new demographic group that did not exist.

A lack of differentiation is another factor that diminishes brands over time. That's what happened to Oldsmobile, at one time a top-selling car. What was an Oldsmobile versus a Buick or a Chevrolet? The distinctions were so minute that, over time, Oldsmobile was squeezed out.

To avoid such a fate, companies must continue investing in their brands to keep them updated, energized, and differentiated. When brands believe they are in an unassailable position, they are usually one wrong move away from meltdown.

There are plenty of examples of brands that get it right. Nike has kept in touch with its customers and expanded its brand from trainers to include other categories of sports clothing and equipment. So successful has it been that it has survived occasional bouts of poor publicity about its manufacturing processes; Nike is still seen as a tick of approval by its devotees.

Brands such as Sony and Campbell's Soup constantly invest in product innovation. Even the image of Betty Crocker on food packages has been updated over the decades so that she always looks contemporary.

But it remains an uphill struggle to energize a brand if its category is dying. This is often the most serious challenge that brand designers face.

2

2
Another brand facing category problems is Cadillac, because the brand is perceived as having problems with its standard of luxury overbalancing the cars' performance and economy.

3
Mazda is a good example of a revitalized brand. It grew close to its customers, updated its personality with chic sports models such as the Miata, and rethought its internal culture to impressive effect. But it never lost sight of its Far Eastern roots, with all their associations of high-tech style and efficiency.

1
With an increasing number of people turning to filmless digital photography (which allows people to print their own color photos), Kodak was forced to reposition its historically film-based business and start manufacturing its own range of digital cameras.

3

BRAND VALUATION

The simple definition of the value of a brand (or the brand equity) is the amount another party is prepared to pay for it. Often this bears little relation to profitability. Recently, many of the brands with the greatest perceived value were Internet ventures—despite the fact that many of the companies concerned were nowhere near returning a profit. The brands were seen as the definitive players in a new market—thanks mainly to good branding design supporting a clearly identified business opportunity.

Another way of calculating the value of a brand is to look at the difference between the amount paid to buy a company, and the monetary value of that company's fixed assets. This difference represents the "good will" being purchased, which is usually a reflection of the perceived value of the company's key products or brands.

The Internet space in particular has seen brand valuations often vastly exceed those of long-established brands with strong revenue streams, healthy growth, and good profit forecasts.

Many companies have had to build the infrastructure to support a good piece of brand design, and an attractive interface. Their extraordinary brand equity for several years demonstrated, if nothing else, the value to the market of defining a new territory, and creating a unique piece of brand design to stake their claim on it.

There are a number of financial companies that offer advice on how best to manage a brand and how to accurately gauge the value of a brand. This page, from the PriceWaterhouse-Coopers website, provides some idea as to how such companies go about assessing and managing brands.

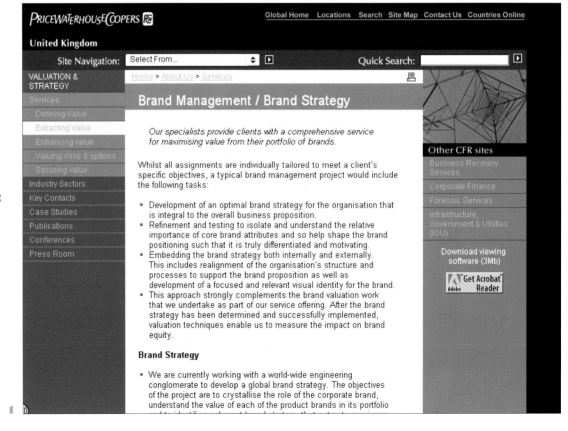

2 | 3 | 4
Amazon, Google, and ebay have, in a relatively short space of time, become household names in most industrial countries. All three are good examples of companies whose brands are valued at more than their assets and annual turnover.

COMMODITY BRANDING

Manufacturers of raw materials and commodity products often ignore the opportunity to increase their margins, create consumer demand for their products, and build value by employing the branding practices made successful by many consumer packaged goods enterprises.

Intel, with its "Intel Inside" strategy, branded its microprocessor through computer manufacturers directly to the end-user, turning microprocessors into a significant selling point for every computer. While greatly increasing the value of its microprocessors, Intel's branding strategy also built brand equity—valued in 2000 at $34.67 billion on sales of $33.7 billion.

The pharmaceutical industry started branding pharmaceuticals directly to the consumer, creating consumer choice and demand through informative consumer advertising campaigns. These have transformed a "direct-to-doctor" marketplace into one that is driven by consumer demand.

The makers of commodity products often assume that branding and marketing their products is impossible. Or they believe that branding is too complex and too expensive to be worthwhile.

"Branded raw materials," such as basic drugs, bring greater value to both manufacturer and end user, while also increasing profit margins. By branding raw materials, manufacturers increase the perception of their products by offering the added ingredient of good quality. Consumers experience greater satisfaction by purchasing such a product, because of the implied guarantee.

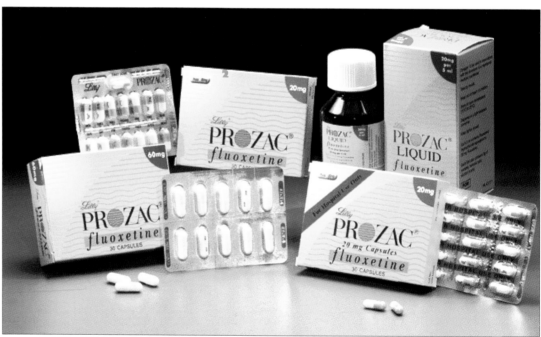

1

Research shows that most people are much more familiar with the antidepressant brand Prozac than they are with the actual drug, fluoxetine. This illustrates the strength of a well-managed branding campaign.

3

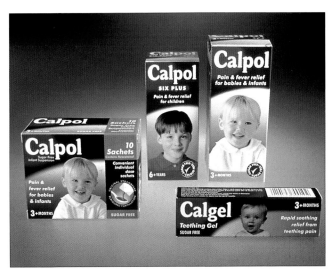

4

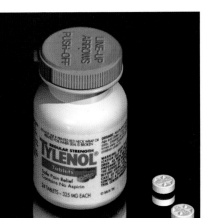

5

2
The fruit and fruit juice retailer Del Monte has, over a number of print and television advertising campaigns, forged a relationship with the consumer that is based on trust. Del Monte is perceived as choosing only the best-quality fruit for its products.

3 | 4 | 5
Listerine, Calpol, and Tylenol are, in those countries where the products are available, recognized as brands that are effective and reassuring. The branding secret is to get people to ask for the product by product name rather than by its generic equivalent.

Branded goods are a subtle form of brand design. They create trust, assist shopping and purchase, build brand loyalty, steal market share from other players, fend off the threat of new entrants to the market, and create financial success.

Brand design in this sector provides a good strategy, which is often overlooked, of overcoming decreasing margins in the sale of commodity products, while also building a sustainable competitive advantage for long-term success.

COBRANDING—THE RULES

Cobranding is where two or more branded products (constituent brands) join forces to form a separate and unique product (a composite brand). This is a strategy popular when introducing new consumer products.

Recent marketplace examples include Kudo's Granola bars with Snicker's pieces, the Ford Explorer with an Eddie Bauer interior, and Betty Crocker Brownie Mix with Hershey's chocolate flavoring, while McDonald's has joined forces with Cadbury's in the UK and Oreo in the US to create a range of dessert products.

There are many different types of cobranding strategies. Joint promotions represent an attempt by one or both brands to secure corporate endorsements that will improve their respective market positions (such as McDonald's and Disney).

Joint advertising, meanwhile, is a more precise technique. Bacardi and Coca-Cola promote the complementary use of their products, reflecting a common, popular choice. More creative examples include Apple's Powerbook campaign, which featured the movie *Mission Impossible*, or the more recent Nokia campaign with the Steven Spielberg film *Minority Report*.

The latter example was clever, as the film was implicitly critical of communications technologies, but Nokia still gained kudos by implying that its current technologies were futuristic and were creating a communications revolution.

Physical product integration takes place when one branded product is inextricably linked with another. Consumer product manufacturers are increasingly interested in cobranding strategies as a means of gaining greater marketplace exposure, fending off the threat of private label brands, and sharing high promotional costs with a partner.

The cobranded product is new to the consumer, even though the constituent brand names are not. Therefore, consumers use the constituent brand names to make judgments about the cobranded product in the absence of further information.

However, one danger of cobranding is the possibility that consumers might transfer a negative experience with one constituent brand to the other partner. Cobranding can undermine a brand's positioning when consumers blame the wrong brand for their dissatisfaction.

Another type of cooperative marketing program is "tie-ins." Film, video, game, music, and book publishing all benefit from this. The successes of Harry Potter and the *Star Wars* films have opened up opportunities for a wide range of companies to join forces and extend the experience far beyond the original book or film. Drinks, sweets, toiletries, and toy manufacturers have all helped extend these globe-conquering franchises.

Walkers, the British snack company, launched a special limited edition of potato chips called "Great British Flavours" in 2001.

This range brought together Walkers' chips and traditional British brands: Branston Pickle, Heinz Ketchup, and Marmite.

2 | 3 | 4
Brands in a variety of categories, from cellphones to fast food, have used cobranding to push sales and improve loyalty among their customers.

DESIGNING EXHIBITIONS

Designing exhibitions, fairs, shows, and displays is an important aspect of a brand's presence today. More often than not, people form their view of a brand by the way in which it presents itself to potential customers.

Displaying products has been an important means of selling products since trading began. From the earliest markets to today's expensive trade fairs, the concept has changed little. What has changed, though, is the sophistication of the display.

Let's review the design issues for some key types of displays that brand owners are likely to use. The four most common display types are exhibitions for consumers, trade fairs, flagship stores or branches, and in-store merchandising.

The most important elements for designers to understand when creating an effective and striking exhibition are: "the story," headings, hierarchies, labels and captions, the copy, presentation, print (weight and spacing), scale and distance, rhythm and consistency, type production, order, decoration, and composition. All should conform to the brand's values, ethos, and visual identity.

Trade fairs are an important way to show off a brand to customers, partners, investors—and, also important, to competitors. Most brand owners hire a shell that looks just like everyone else's, but which, with careful design, striking images, some give-away incentives, planning, and execution can be converted into a powerful medium for displaying the brand's values to all.

1 | 2

Displaying products and services has been a technique used by all industries for a long time, but the sophistication and technology behind the exhibitions and trade fairs have come a long way.

3

4

3 | 4
Signage and
presentation
mean everything
in exhibitions and,
indeed, public spaces.
Signage must convey
information effectively
and attractively, while
retaining the general
style and atmosphere
of the space. Innovation
is also important. This
winter collection of
handbags has been
set in resin to resemble
ice cubes.

VIRAL MARKETING

During the earlier discussion on guerrilla marketing (*see* page 106), we touched briefly on viral marketing; this describes any strategy that encourages individuals to pass on a marketing message to others, creating the potential for exponential growth in the message's exposure and influence.

Like viruses, such strategies take advantage of rapid multiplication to explode the message to thousands, or even to millions. Off the Internet, viral marketing has been variously referred to as "word-of-mouth," "creating a buzz," "leveraging the media," and "network marketing." On the Internet the effect can be vast, and sometimes uncontrollable.

Two of the most successful examples of viral marketing have been Hotmail and Yahoo! mail. The strategy for both was simple:
• Give away free email addresses and services.
• Attach a simple tag at the bottom of every free message sent: "Get your private, free email at..."
• Stand back while people email to their own networks of friends and associates.
• Watch the process snowball and replicate as thousands of people contact thousands more, and so on.

Some viral marketing strategies work better than others, and few work as well as the simple email strategy. But below are the six basic elements you should consider including in your strategy. A viral marketing strategy need not contain all these elements, but the more of them it embraces, the more powerful the results are likely to be.

An effective viral marketing strategy:
• Gives away products or services.
• Provides for effortless transfer to others.
• Scales easily from small to very large.
• Exploits common motivations and behaviors.
• Utilizes existing communication networks.
• Takes advantage of others' resources.

"Free" is the most powerful word in a marketer's vocabulary. Most viral marketing strategies give away valuable or attractive products, services, or content to attract attention. Free email, free information, free buttons, free software programs that perform powerful functions (but which encourage you to buy the full versions) are all good examples.

The medium that carries your marketing message must be easy to transfer and replicate. Viral marketing

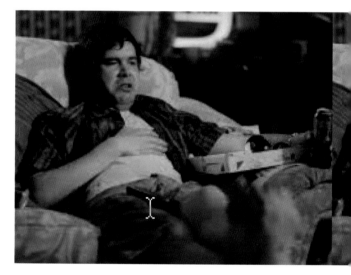

works so well on the Internet because instant communication has become both simple and inexpensive. Also, Internet users like to discover new things and send them to their friends, so if a viral campaign can give the impression of being "discovered" rather than forced down people's throats, then it stands the greatest chance of success.

Digital formats make copying simple. From a marketing standpoint, you must simplify your marketing message so that it can be transmitted easily and without degradation.

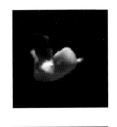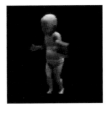
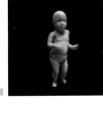

1

The "dancing baby" was one of the earliest examples of viral marketing. Although not actually used to advertise any specific product, hundreds of thousands of people downloaded the animation to view on their computers within weeks of it becoming available.

2

This 30-second film was made and optimized for Web use by the UK marketing company, Viral Factory. They specialize in creating amusing films that people will email to one another. Here the sequence was created for a new brand of Ford car.

3

Yahoo! were among the first to utilize the concept of viral marketing to launch their email service.

125

the all-new ford**fiesta**

2

3

Personalize   Finance   Shop   YAHOO!®   Email

 Yahoo! Personals - find your match. post a free ad. take a tour. create an ema

| Search | • advanced search • most popular |

ew! **Yahoo! Mail Plus** - Powerful. Affordable. Sign up now   **Yahoo! Autos**

BRAND CREATION—THE PROCESS

Most companies' branding activities are carried out by external agencies but controlled by an in-house manager. The agency's responsibilities will vary from brand to brand, but generally they will monitor how the brand is performing, implement brand strategy, and ensure that the brand is accurately represented across various media, or 'channels'. This illustration shows some of the key people involved in brand creation.

COMPANY

Brand Owner

The brand owner ensures that the brand is interpreted correctly within the company and externally, and also works with the agency to ensure the brand stays fresh and relevant.

Marketing Manager

His/her role is to work with the brand owner to create 'on-brand' communications, so that all key messages are appropriate to the brand's identity.

AGENCY

Partner

This is the main contact for the clients. He or she oversees the project.

Brand Consultant

The brand consultant runs the brand project, and is the main source of thinking for the brand strategy.

Art Director

This role oversees the creative direction of the work being done, whether it's the name, the logo or the implementation of the brand in specific projects.

Producer

The producer works closely with the project manager to ensure that all the creative work being done to the right level and standard.

User Specialist

This role is about defining how the brand needs to be translated into a 'user experience' on various channels, such as the Web, print, TV, or radio.

Copywriter

He or she forms and produces the language, style and tone of all the words that the brand sends out.

In this context, the designer creates visual representations of the work that the strategist does and creates appropriate imagery and 'mood boards'.

Project Manager

This person ensures that the work is being done on time and to budget, and that all schedules and people involved with the brand are being properly managed.

Designer

The information design specialist creates bills, invoices, statements and so on, that are easy to comprehend for the customer, and which provide useful brand information, extensions, and marketing opportunities.

Information Designer

❶ Business idea and plan in place
❷ Naming strategy and name
❸ Logo strategy and visual representation
❹ Visual identity standards and guidelines
❺ Voice programs
❻ Voice applications

❙

This illustration and key show the basic procedures that are undertaken during the creation of a brand. Once the product has been 'green lit' (1) the next stage is to arrive at an appropriate name for the product or service (2). With the name in place, the visual representation of the brand is devised (3). Following this, guidelines for usage are devised (4), before the strategy of placing and exposing the brand is finalized (5, 6).

OPENING UP SHELL

Shell has been using the *Pecten*, or scallop, symbol for more than 100 years. The logo's characteristic red and yellow colors have defined not just the company's business objectives, but also Shell's stated values of quality and reliability.

That said, as these pages demonstrate, the company's logo has evolved a great deal over the last 100 years, even though Shell would maintain that its ideals have remained constant.

Shell uses the same logo, colors, and brand around the world for all its marketing and advertising. This single brand philosophy not only helps to promote a "united front," but is based on the company's vision of being an environmentally and socially responsible organization. As we review the brand's history, we can see the development and shift in corporate thinking, and how that is represented in the brand design.

The exact form of the Shell emblem has changed gradually over the years in line with trends in graphic design. The current version was created by the designer Raymond Loewy and introduced in 1971. Thirty years on it stands the test of time as one of the world's most recognized symbols. Like the scallop shell itself, the colors have also been modified over the years, most notably in 1995 when a bright, fresh, and more consumer friendly "Shell Red" and "Shell Yellow" were introduced to launch Shell's new retail visual identity.

1930

1948

Brand timeline

1891

The word "Shell" first appeared as the trademark for kerosene being shipped to the Far East by Marcus Samuel and Company. This London-based business used to deal with antiques and oriental seashells. They were so popular that the company made a huge profit from their sales.

1897

The word "Shell" was elevated to corporate status in 1897, when Samuel formed The Shell Transport and Trading Company.

1901

The first logo (1901) was a mussel shell, but by 1904 a scallop shell had been introduced as a visual manifestation of the corporate and brand name.

1904

Both the word "Shell" and the scallop symbol may have been suggested to Samuel and Company by another interested party. A Mr. Graham, who imported Samuel's kerosene into India and sold it as "Graham's Oil," poured capital into, and became a director of, The Shell Transport

and Trading Company. There is some evidence that the shell emblem was taken from his family coat of arms. The "St. James' Shell" had been adopted by the Graham family after its ancestors made the pilgrimage to Santiago de Compostella in northern Spain. The original design was a reasonably faithful reproduction of the *Pecten* or scallop shell.

1907

Royal Dutch Petroleum Company and "Shell" Transport and Trading merged and decided to take on a shorter form of the name (Shell) and the scallop emblem for the new Royal Dutch/Shell Group.

1901

1904

1909

1955

1961

1971

1915

When the US operation, the Shell Company of California, first built service stations, it had to compete against other companies. Bright colors were the solution, but these had to be colors that would suit Californians.

The accepted explanation is that because of the state's strong Spanish connections, the red and yellow of Spain were chosen. Samuel and Company, however, had first shipped kerosene to the Far East in tins painted red.

The changing face of the Shell logo.

1995

1999

THINKING DIFFERENTLY

Apple's history is the definitive rollercoaster ride of a new technology company. There have been many highs and lows since the company started in Steve Jobs' bedroom in the 1960s. But the bedrock of Apple's history has been design innovation in every aspect of its product line, from its heyday in the 1980s through the dark years of the mid-1990s to its renaissance at the end of that decade.

Unusually for a technology company, Apple is an aspirational, lifestyle brand, as well as a functional one with hardcore, professional fans. Apple computer has not only developed numerous new products, it has also built a reputation for quality and reliability among designers and media people, a good route to the wider population's affections.

132

1
The reknowned apple logo has evolved since its conception, from an apple without the famous bite taken out of it, through the rainbow-colored apple with the bite, to the single-color logo we know today.

2

Brand timeline

1976
Steve Wozniak designed the Apple I. Jobs' inspiration for the name Apple came from the Beatles' record label, Apple Corps, in the 1960s. Like many of the Silicon Valley crowd, the two Steves were very much children of the 1960s. Jobs and Wozniak were stuck for a name for their new company, and decided that if they couldn't think of one that was better than Apple, then they would choose Apple. The rest is history.

1981
Wozniak left the company and Jobs became chairman of Apple Computer in March. At this time, IBM released the first Personal Computer (PC).

1983
John Sculley, then president of Pepsi-Cola, was brought in to help the company "grow up" and become more marketing focused.

1984
Apple introduced the Macintosh (the Apple Mac), a design-led machine with a graphical user interface (GUI). Although the operating system was an immediate hit, the idea of "windows"-style functionality was not entirely original; the underlying concept originated in research carried out by Xerox at its PARC facility. Of course, Microsoft also developed a similar idea with Windows. Apple premiered the Mac with the iconic "1984" TV advertising campaign, suggesting that it wanted to smash the tyranny of big, corporate computing.

1985
Jobs tried to oust Sculley but failed. Jobs resigned the same day, leaving Sculley as the head of Apple Computer.

1

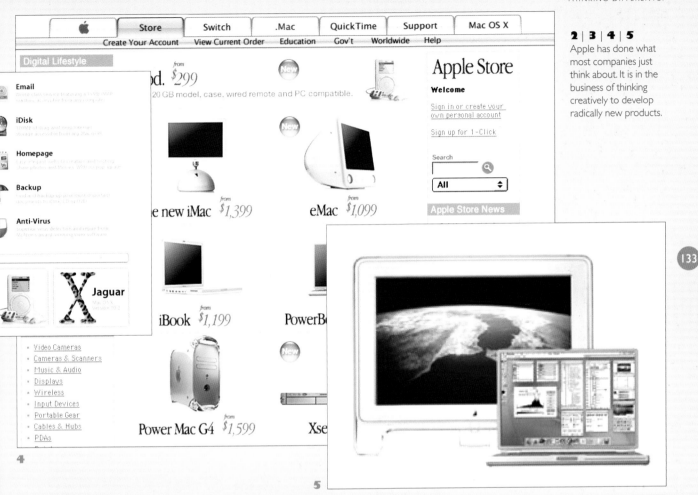

Apple has done what most companies just think about. It is in the business of thinking creatively to develop radically new products.

133

4

5

1991

Apple released its first generation of PowerBooks, ahead of the buyers' market. Work was started on a personal digital assistant (PDA), which Apple called the Newton. At the time, though, the idea did not catch on; again, it was far ahead of a market that was still growing accustomed to PCs. (Alas, the Newton fell on Apple's head.) Apple's woes were mounting: it failed to license its operating system to other makers, allowing Microsoft to storm the market and begin relegating Apple machines to a minority market.

1997

Steve Jobs returns as "interim CEO" to reverse Apple's steep decline. He saw refocusing the brand on its innovative, design-led origins as the only solution. He launched an aggressive advertising campaign for a new range of Macs. He also strengthened his alliance with Microsoft (which had continued to make software packages in Mac versions). Office '98 was available for the Mac by the year's end.

1998

Apple stores were launched, as was an entirely new Mac design—the iMac. This quickly became a design classic, integrating everything bar the keyboard into a single, eye-catching, colorful unit. The message was clear: smash the tyranny of the gray and boring PC once again.

1999

Apple introduced the iBook laptop, based on the same principles that had made the iMac so popular a year earlier.

2001

Apple announced a new line of PowerMacs with CD-RW drives and announced two new applications: iDVD, a DVD-authoring program; and iTunes, which allowed users to encode and listen to MP3s. Apple extended this functionality by announcing its first non-computer product in several years, the iPod.

2002

Apple radically redesigned the iMac so that it barely resembled a computer, and introduced an equally radical new operating system, OS X.

DIFFERENT THINGS FOR DIFFERENT PEOPLE

One of the most familiar brands of our times continues to be Virgin. Arguably, Richard Branson's greatest skill is as a brand builder and brand publicist. He has stretched the Virgin brand to boundaries that people didn't believe any single brand could reach.

Virgin remains the glue that holds an ever-expanding group of businesses together. In an interview in *Vogue* as far back as 1968 Branson said, "I want to create a company which will do all sorts of different things for different people. It doesn't matter what we're doing, it's the way we are going to do it that is going to matter." He created a brand that does exactly that.

From the mid 1980s when the original record company became truly profitable, Virgin expanded into a large number of businesses, keeping the values of the brand consistent, while applying them in whichever way best suited the markets in which they operated.

Virgin today is made up of over 200 companies, under complex ownership, employing around 30,000 people.

Virgin ensures that each new venture it enters shares the ethos of the main brand: value for money,

innovation, quality, fun, and exceptional service. Branson's personality is an important ingredient in delivering the promise.

When the first Virgin Atlantic Airways flight took off, Branson appeared in the cockpit wearing a leather World War I flight helmet. For the launch of Virgin Bride he arrived in a wedding dress, and at the US launch of Virgin Mobile in 2002 he wore a muscle suit and sat on a giant mobile phone.

All the stunts pulled by Branson and Virgin brands are meant to excite and surprise consumers. More importantly, they guarantee column inches in the press.

Brand timeline

1968
Richard Branson started his first business—a student magazine.

1970
The first Virgin business was launched: a small mail-order record retailer.

1972
Virgin Records was set up in 1972 by Branson and his cousin, Simon Draper. The unexpected success of 19-year-old Mike Oldfield's debut release, "Tubular Bells," gave Branson's ambitions a massive boost. At the time, the Virgin Records logo was a very 1970s image of two naked women intertwined.

1981
The familiar Virgin typography and logo were introduced.

1983
Film and video distribution was started as Virgin Vision and Virgin Games.

1984
Virgin Atlantic was launched, followed by Virgin Holidays.

1991
Virgin Megastores were set up, along with Virgin Publishing.

1992
Branson sold Virgin Records to Thorn EMI.

1996
Virgin acquired Euro Belgian Airlines and renamed it Virgin Express. The V2 music label and music publishing business was set up; Virgin.net was launched. Virgin Bride also launched, and Virgin won a cross-country passenger rail franchise in the UK.

2

3

4

5

6

1997
Cosmetic range Virgin Vie premiered.

1999
Virgin Mobile was launched.

2000
V.Shop was launched.

2002
Virgin Active (fitness centers) was launched.

1 | 2 | 3 | 4 | 5 | 6
From trains, planes, and records to soft drinks, weddings, and cellphones, Virgin's disparate group of companies are held together by the same company ethos—price, quality, a sense of fun—and of course the ubiquitous logo.

THE COOLEST OF KICKS

1

When Adidas entered the market about 50 years ago, its focus was on producing shoes made specifically for soccer and running. Establishing the brand as the choice for professional athletes eventually led them to become a mainstream sportswear brand.

In the 1980s, rap and hip hop band Run DMC enhanced Adidas' street reputation with the rap "My Adidas" paying respect to their favorite shell-toe. But by the early '90s, Nike and Reebok were beating Adidas— even in Germany, its home turf.

The next generation of Adidas shoes took the company back to the core values that Adidas derived from sport: authenticity, inspiration, and commitment. However, the real key to success in the now-crowded market lay in the considerable endorsement deals that Adidas developed with world-class athletes. Recent sports figures representing Adidas score highly in the celebrity stakes. British soccer superstar David Beckham's relationship with Adidas has had a massive impact on Adidas' profile in the UK.

In the US, Kobe Bryant is another Adidas endorsee. The LA Laker and youngest NBA "All-Star" player is a

5

Brand timeline

1927
Brothers Adi and Rudi Dassler set up their first shoe factory with 25 people. Three years later Adi Dassler bought the factory.

1928
Dassler shoes were worn at the Olympic Games for the first time.

1931
Dassler Tennis shoes were launched.

1936
Jessie Owens won four gold medals wearing Dassler shoes.

1938
Adi bought his second production facility in Herzogenaurach.

1948
Adi and Rudi split up. Adi created Adidas, Rudi created Puma. Adidas registered the famous three stripes design.

1952
Adidas were the most popular shoes worn at the Olympics in Helsinki. Emil Zatopek won three medals wearing Adidas shoes.

1954
West Germany won the soccer world cup wearing Adidas shoes with revolutionary screw-in studs.

1960
Adidas was the dominant brand in the Olympic Games in Rome, with 75 percent of the athletes wearing Adidas shoes.

1962
Adidas launched a range of sporting accessories, including balls and clothes.

1972
The "Trefoil" logo was introduced. The three leaves symbolized the Olympic spirit. Adidas became official supplier of the Munich Olympics.

1974
West Germany won the soccer world cup again, with most players wearing Adidas boots.

adidas®

2

1 | 2 | 3 | 4

By distancing themselves from the fashion business and returning to their core values of authentic sportswear, helped by the endorsement of celebrities such as French soccer star Patrick Viera, Adidas have won back a significant market share.

5

The shoe worn by Jesse Owens when he ran the 1936 Berlin Olympics.

massively popular athlete. This translates directly into sales. Equally compelling is Russian-born, American-bred tennis star Anna Kournikova.

Reinvention was key. On its website, Adidas acknowledges, "The markets and industry in which we compete are transforming rapidly, paced by the evolution—or revolution—in how 'sports' are defined. Team sports such as soccer and basketball will always be a fundamental part of sporting competition. Today, however, eclectic, individual, 'no-rules' sports such as snowboarding, inline skating, and surfing have grown into significant categories."

1978

Adi Dassler died. His wife Kathe Dassler continued to run the business.

1984

Kathe died, leaving the business to her son Horst Dassler.

1987

Stefi Graf won Wimbledon while on a contract with Adidas. Horst Dassler died at the young age of 51. The company faced difficult times.

1990

Adidas became incorporated and Bernard Tapie bought 80 percent of the stock.

1995

Adidas went public.

1996

Adidas revitalized itself with a campaign:"We knew then, we know now." A new logo was launched.

1997

Adidas modernized its face with endorsements from David Beckham, Anna Kournikova, and others.

2001

Herbert Hainer became CEO.

4

FROM TRAVELER'S CHECKS TO THE BLUE CARD

American Express began life in 1850 as a regional freight express business. In 1882 the company took a small step that became the genesis of a dramatic strategic shift. Due to the increasingly popular postal money order, American Express faced declining demand for its cash shipping services. In response, American Express created its own money order. The Express Money Order became an unexpected success.

A decade later in 1892, the American Express president took a vacation in Europe and found it hard to translate his letters of credit into cash. This initiated the idea of creating the American Express traveler's check. The new product created the perfect launch pad for the company to enter financial services.

The next logical step was for American Express to enter travel services. All of these small steps created a giant leap away from the company's founding concept of being a freight express business.

AmEx, as it is popularly known, is now a truly global brand offering products and

services in nearly every country in the world. The classic green AmEx card was launched in 1958 and, over the decades, the card evolved to reflect its consumers' changing lifestyles and aspirations.

However, with technological change moving ever faster, American Express' core products have proved less relevant to a new cyber-savvy generation of consumers. The company realized that it needed to attract 25–40 year olds, a market that the traditional green card had never been able to win over. Any credit card company can attract new customers, if not their loyalty, by offering low interest rates. But rather than compete on those terms, American Express decided to reinvent the entire credit card category. The result: Blue, a credit card that breaks the mold in functionality, by offering reward points, no annual fee, and a security chip.

Many companies do not consider the fact that a branded card can be the most frequent contact a customer has with a brand. Cards are badges symbolizing status, aspirations, affinities, and personal preferences.

Brand timeline

1850

Founded by Henry G. Wells, William G. Fargo, and John Butterfield, American Express was originally an express freight company.

1860s

American Express transported vital supplies to Union Army depots and conducted the high-risk task of delivering election ballots to troops in the field.

1882

"Money Order" was created as a safer option of transferring money.

1886

American Express established relationships with banks across Europe, allowing emigrants to the United States to transfer money to their families.

1891

American Express introduced American Express traveler's checks.

1914–18

American Express offices helped US customers trapped in Europe during the war to get back home safely. After the war American Express expanded their travel organization globally.

1963

American Express launched its first green charge card in the UK.

1970

American Express launched the corporate card.

1996

American Express launched its first credit card in the UK.

138

1
The modern-day green card campaign uses the strap line "live green," and with it a series of striking visuals by celebrated photographer David Stewart.

2 | 3 | 4
A brand's cards can be used to signal a change in positioning, such as the AmEx Blue card featured here. It can also be used to sponsor the values of other brands.

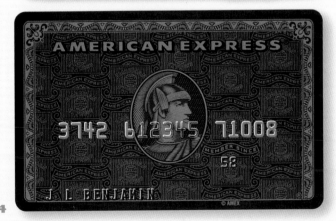

THE SWEDISH AFFAIR

The Swedish furniture company is beyond doubt a great retail brand. It has created a bond with young, price-conscious homemakers in 39 countries. To these people IKEA—with its assembly from flat packs—represents elegant design at reasonable prices. To the loyal customers who fill its stores, IKEA is stylish self-assembly.

Rising from its humble origins in Småland, a rural area of Sweden, IKEA grew from a tiny mail-order business to a multibillion-dollar furniture giant with more than 150 stores and 39,000 employees. The brand is driven by the sometimes eccentric philosophies of its founder, Ingvar Kamprad. The company name bears the initials of the farm and his home community—I(ngvar), K(amprad), E(imtaryad—the farm), and A(gunnaryd—the community).

IKEA aims to give all its customers good-quality, highly practical, contemporary design at affordable prices. IKEA's mission statement distills its functional objectives: "To contribute to a better everyday working life for the majority of people, by offering a wide range of home furnishings items of good design and function, at prices so low that the majority of people can afford to buy them."

1 | 2 | 3 | 4 | 5
Many consider a visit to IKEA as a day out for the whole family. The interiors are well laid out, the range is ample and diverse, the prices are low, and most products are in stock and can be taken home straightaway.

2

1

140

Brand timeline

1943
Ingvar registered the IKEA name, and began selling pens, watches, jewelry, and wallets.

1946
The first advertisement for IKEA appeared.

1950
IKEA added furniture to its range and started to sell it at factory prices by mail order. Suppliers were threatened with boycotts and IKEA was literally thrown out of the big furniture trade fair in Stockholm.

1951
The first IKEA catalog was issued followed by the first permanent showroom, in Älmhult in 1953.

1955
IKEA started to design its own furniture.

1956
The company launched its definitive flat packs for all its furniture.

1959
Gillis Lundgren—the fourth employee at IKEA—designed TORE, one of Ikea's best-selling storage systems.

1960
The IKEA "experience" was established: a large warehouse-style store selling furniture and home accessories, where customers serve themselves and the goods are available to take home that day.

1963
The first IKEA store not located in Sweden opened outside Oslo.

1965
The first store opened in Stockholm.

1973
A store opened near Zurich. Its success paved the way for expansion from Switzerland into Germany.

Brand values and informal rules are strong and ever-present elements that help create a bond between IKEA coworkers worldwide. In 1976 Ingvar Kamprad described these elements in what later became known as "The Testament of a Furniture Dealer." Everybody working with the IKEA concept knows and understands this document, and according to Ingvar Kamprad, maintaining a strong IKEA culture is one of the most crucial factors behind the continued success of the brand.

IKEA has a rigid system of how and why it includes a product in its range. It achieves this through following the principles of what it calls "Democratic Design." Any item that enters the IKEA range must meet the criteria set down under the following three headings: Form, Function, and Price. Is it pleasing to the eye? Does it serve the purpose for which it is intended? Is it good value for money? If the answer is "no" to any of these questions, then the company believes it has no place in the IKEA range.

1976

Ingvar Kamprad wrote "The Testament of a Furniture Dealer." The first IKEA store in Canada opened.

1983

The 6,000th employee joined IKEA.

1985

The United States received its first Ikea store.

1987

The first IKEA store in the UK opened.

1993

IKEA opened its 114th store (in 25 countries).

1997

IKEA introduced Children's IKEA.

1999

Ingvar Kamprad initiated the "Big Thank You Event" as a millennium reward to the workers within the IKEA group. The total of all sales worldwide was given to the employees—on average a month's salary.

HOW FAR CAN IT GO?

If someone had said to the pharmacist in Newcastle in 1927 who made a drink for child convalescence that it would one day be available in trendy gyms in London, and be sold not in pharmacies, but in supermarkets, he would not have believed it. But that's exactly what has happened to Lucozade. From the crinkly orange cellophane-covered bottles to the current portable, recreation-friendly sport pack, this brand has broken dozens of supposed brand barriers.

142

1 | 2 | 3 | 4
Once considered suitable for young children recovering from minor illness, Lucozade is now a massive lifestyle brand, used by sportsmen and women to improve performance, and promoted by Lara Croft, the world's biggest game icon.

1

2

Brand timeline

1927
Lucozade was developed by a British pharmacist for child convalescence. It was distributed, mainly in pharmacies, by Beecham.

1979
The drink was repositioned as a pick-me-up for otherwise healthy people who felt run down.

1980
The 250 ml (8 fl oz) and 1 litre (2 pint) glass bottle were introduced. Distribution was extended to supermarkets, grocers, and news agents.

1983
The brand was repositioned as "Lucozade replaces lost energy." The UK Olympic athlete Daley Thompson fronted a marketing campaign, increasing sales over six years by 300 percent.

1986
Orange and lemon barley flavors were introduced in 250 ml (8 fl oz) and 1 litre (2 pint) glass bottles and 330 ml (11 fl oz) cans.

1990
Lucozade Sport was launched, fronted by English soccer star John Barnes. The product was awarded the most successful soft drinks launch prize for 1990–91.

1992
Lucozade Sport became the Official Sport Drink of the soccer players' league in the UK. The Lucozade Sport range was extended to include a lemon/lime flavor, and Orange Sportpack was launched.

Timeline Source: Brand Strategy, March 2002, Issue 157

1995

Lucozade NRG was launched. Lucozade Sport became the official sponsor of the English rugby team. Orange 500ml (18 fl oz) bottle was launched.

1996

Lucozade was repositioned from "replaces lost energy" to simply "energy boost." At this point the products' visual identities were radically changed.

1997

England's soccer captain Alan Shearer appeared as brand ambassador in Lucozade Sport advertising.

1998

Lucozade Energy was relaunched with a new advertising push, new pack graphics, and a 500ml (18 fl oz) plastic bottle. Lucozade Sport's positioning was changed to "Improves sporting performance." The "Keep going 33 percent longer" claim was introduced.

1999

A multimedia campaign for Lucozade NRG—starring computer heroine Lara Croft—was launched.
Lucozade Low Calorie was relaunched, moving away from "healthy diet drinks" to "low calorie energy drink."

2000–1

James Cracknell (Olympic rower), Matt Dawson (England rugby), Jason Queally (Olympic cyclist), and Tim Don (triathlete) joined as brand ambassadors.

2002

England soccer star Michael Owen joined Team Lucozade Sport. Lucozade Sport began a 5-year deal as Official Sport drink of the Flora London Marathon. Lucozade Sport carbo gel was launched.

GO CREATE

Initially established as "Totsuken" (Tokyo Tsushin Kenkujo), Sony's two founders, Akio Morita and Masaru Ibuka, decided that to make the company more accessible to the West the name had to change. Sony was derived from the Latin word *sonus*—the root of words such as "sound" and "sonic'—and Sony's earliest product was a tape recorder. The word was also used to express Sony's ethos of promoting entertainment, youthfulness, and invention.

In fact the whole culture at Sony is based around providing their technicians with a good working environment and the time to innovate and think "out of the box." There is no better proof of this than the fact that Sony's two most successful product ranges, the Walkman and the PlayStation, were both developed in-house. Both products have created significant revolutions and cultural shifts in the way music and home entertainment are created and consumed.

Sony's motivation has always been having deep consumer insight into the ways in which consumers wish to be entertained. Walkman and its dozens of spin-offs are not about technology, but about delivering the benefit of listening to music on the move.

144

1 | 2 | 3
Sony's vision is that entertainment content (which Sony owns) will be piped into your PlayStation2 (which Sony makes), and then played on your TV or stereo (which Sony also makes).

4
Sony is extending brand recognition by adding branded clothing to its range of products.

Brand timeline

1945
Following World War II, founder Masaru Ibuka returned to Tokyo and set up a radio repair center. By October, Ibuka and his group had established a new facility, called "Tokyo Tsushin Kenkyujo" (Totsuken), or "Tokyo Telecommunications Research Institute."

1946
More than 20 management and staff attended the inauguration ceremony which officially established Tokyo Tsushin Kogyo (Totsuko).

1950
"G-Type," Japan's first tape recorder, was launched by Totsuko.

1955
"TR-55," Japan's first transistor radio, was launched.

1958
A new departure for Totsuko as it adopted "Sony" as its corporate name. It was certainly an innovative step. At the time it was highly unusual for a Japanese company to spell its name in Roman letters (or, as when "Sony" is written in Japanese, in phonetic script rather than Chinese characters).

Product timeline

1960
The world's first direct-view transistor television was produced.

1963
Sony made the world's first transistor, compact- sized, VCR.

1968
The "Trinitron" color TV was launched.

1975
The "Betamax" VCR for home use first made.

1979
The first "Walkman" was launched.

1982
Sony produced its first CD player.

1985
A single-unit, 8mm video camera was made.

1987
Sony launched its first Digital Audio Tape (DAT) deck.

1988
"Mavica," an electronic, still-image camera, was launched.

1990–91

"HD Trinitron," a 36-inch, high-definition color TV, was manufactured.

1992

The first MiniDisc (MD) system appeared.

1994

Sony produced the world's first high-brightness, green light-emitting diode.

1995

Plasmatron, a flat panel display screen, was manufactured, and a format for high-density optical disc was finalized, providing the new format name, DVD.

1996

"VAIO" PC appeared on the market.

1997

DVD video player was launched.

1998

Sony announced the "Memory Stick," a recordable integrated circuit memory card.

1999

Super Audio CD players were first produced, along with the entertainment robot "AIBO."

2000

Sony's Personal Entertainment Organizer "CLIE" was launched. Sony developed the world's first small biped entertainment robot.

2001

Sony demonstrated "Infostick™" and Bluetooth™ module— a form of wireless data exchange.

Timeline Source: www.Sony.net

HAVE YOU HOOVERED?

A young inventor, who worked during the evenings as a cleaner, found that dust gave him asthma attacks. To improve his time at work he invented the first vacuum cleaner. He was James Murray Spangler from Ohio. Out of an old tin soapbox, a fan, a pillowcase, and a broom handle, Spangler created an awkward apparatus that sucked in the dust.

Spangler realized that this "suction sweeper," as he called it, had enormous sales potential. Eventually he sold this design to his cousin's husband, W.H. "Boss" Hoover, who manufactured the "Model 0" in 1908. Hoover, realizing the potential, hired engineers to design new and superior methods of cleaning carpets, and eventually established a design development program in 1909. Hoover went on to develop numerous firsts in the market, including the first disposable paper dustbag. The Hoover family owned the company until the 1940s, after which it became publicly owned. The company's stock was first traded on August 6, 1943.

In 1985, Hoover was acquired by the Chicago Pacific Corporation, and, in 1989, Maytag acquired Chicago Pacific. As a result, Hoover belongs to a family of companies with some of the most prestigious names in home appliances, including Jenn-Air, Blodgett, and Magic Chef.

In the 1990s Hoover suffered in a difficult market from increased competition. Hoover had become the standard to such an extent that the word "Hoover" had become synonymous with "vacuum cleaner" and vacuum cleaning. Hoover's longevity and stability had the adverse effect of creating a suspicion of stagnancy in the market. This was emphasized when inventor James Dyson launched his bagless vacuum cleaners, and his design became a major differentiator. In 1992, in an attempt to claw back market share, Hoover offered its customers free flights. The promotion was so popular that Hoover left many customers unhappy as it couldn't possibly satisfy the massive demand.

After a few difficult years Hoover sold the European brand to Candy SpA of Italy. Two different companies in Europe and America now manage Hoover. Candy SpA has ploughed money into new designs and a better range, and has launched the Discovery model. Hoover today is well on its way back to reclaiming its signpost brand position within stores.

Brand timeline

1907
J.M. Spangler created the first prototype vacuum cleaner.

1908
Spangler sold the design to W.H. Hoover and the "Model 0" was manufactured.

1919
A manufacturing facility was established in England.

1921
Hoover began marketing and selling products around the world.

1942
The Hoover Company ceased manufacturing vacuum cleaners and focused its attention on aiding the war effort.

1943
Company stock was first traded.

1956
The Constellation vacuum cleaner was developed.

1968
A 307,200-square-foot factory was added to the east of the original complex.

147

WindTunnel™ with V2™ Technology

CHOOSE A SECTION · DOWNLOAD SPECIFICATIONS

Make cleaning a little easier!

ABOUT US · PRODUCTS · WHERE TO BUY · SERVICE · ONLINE BUYS · WHAT'S NEW

HURRICANE 350 Series

Model no: ...
Type: Upright bagless

KEY FEATURES:

The most powerful Hoover upright cleaners* (*Independently tested to I.E.C 60312

Unique Hoover Grooming Agitator

Our products suck.

VISTAMEDIA

1985
Hoover was acquired by Chicago Pacific Corporation.

1989
Maytag acquired Chicago Pacific.

1995
The European branch of the Hoover brand was sold to Candy SpA of Italy.

Reward Yourself
Buy $299 or more of Hoover products
Get a $50 Certificate for amazon.com
Rewarding cleaning through August 17

Make cleaning a little easier!

WindTunnel WITH V2 TECHNOLOGY

▷ Hoover Innovation
▷ Learn About . . .
Find An Owner's Manual
Products
Product Registration
▷ Frequently Asked Questions
Purchase Filter Bags
Employment Opportunities
Site Map

Learn More

THE FUTURE'S BRIGHT, THE FUTURE'S ORANGE

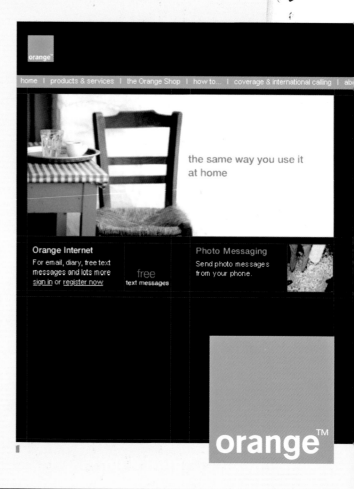

The Europeoan cellphone company Orange was one of the first brands to move cellphone telephony to a new level. A lot of brands today claim to have created their personality through a logo or a symbol, but Orange created theirs with a color and an experience, at a time when that was unheard of in the cellphone world. The idea of per second billing—as started first by Orange—demonstrated their focus on creating value for customers from the very beginning. Orange has managed to persuade customers that technology can be human, and that large telephone operators can listen and be friendly. The brand was launched in 1994, when cellphone telephony was a commodity product and price was the key differentiator.

Orange's strategy has been to build a brand that can be translated across cultures and boundaries in a universal and unique way. It has a reputation for providing the best service, the best-performing network and the best value, as confirmed by many independent industry sources. The market has realized the value of this strategy and now other brands are trying to do what Orange has done from the start—create a brand and an experience that delivers what the brand promises. In Europe, Vodafone, T-Mobile,

Brand timeline

1994

Orange launched as the fourth entrant in the UK cellphone market.

1996

Orange floated on The London Stock Exchange (205 pence/ $3.28 per share) and the NASDAQ; it gained around 500,000 UK customers, 8.5 percent of the UK market.

1996

Orange entered the list of the UK's 100 largest companies.

1997

Orange reached one million UK customers, (14 percent market share). The company announced an £800 million investment plan, aiming to become the UK market leader.

1998

J.D. Power and Associates, the global marketing information services firm, ranked Orange number one in mobile telephone customer satisfaction in the UK.

1999

Orange UK launched "Wildfire," the UK's first voice-activated digital personal assistant. Orange was acquired by the German company Mannesmann.

2000

Vodafone AirTouch plc acquired Mannesmann and undertook to sell Orange. Orange announced agreed acquisition by France Télécom. The majority of France Télécom's cellphone assets were to be combined with those of Orange plc to form an enlarged group, Orange SA.

2000

Orange UK announced the acquisition of Wildfire and Ananova, and a 25 percent stake in NewsTakes— forming the foundations of the Orange Internet platform and OrangeWorld services.

we offer you

Welcome to the Orange **Studio™**, a unique collection of spaces in the centre of Birmingham including an events and exhibitions centre, meeting rooms, a bar, restaurant and roof garden, a graphics bureau, an Internet café and more.

Click here to enter the site

business | today

contact us | search

you want to do?

what is important to you

y on Orange

flirt with Orange Chat

a lot to discover

e your phone online

pay as you go phone

ge move

our latest award

gossip or Chat

and O$_2$ are now moving in that direction. Orange's Brand Director believes that the brand's success is attributable to its complete and unfailing focus on its customers.

One of the unique things about Orange is that it has taken its business and brand strategy and internalized it—not just in its communications business, but across to the call centers, the retail stores, the bills, the people that are customer facing, and their employees. It has not only created a strong external brand (the core elements of which—the logo, the color, and typography—are maintained consistently everywhere they launch) but has filtered these values internally as well. Straightforward, honest, refreshing, dynamic, and friendly are values that are lived internally and demonstrated externally.

Orange promotes its values through advertising and its entire customer-facing communications. This is true not just in the UK, where it is the market leader, but also in countries where the company is still building a reputation. Orange aspires to become a global player and the brand is undoubtedly on its way to achieving that goal.

149

2001

Orange announced "Orange at home." Orange SA successfully completed its flotation, and entered the Paris and London exchanges. Mobilix rebranded as Orange in Denmark; Itineris, OLA, and Mobicarte rebranded as Orange in France.

Don't just talk. See.

Now you can see the faces of your friends and family by receiving or sending photos on an Orange Photo Messaging phone. Visit www.orange.co.uk/photomessaging, call 0800 80 10 80 or contact your Orange stockist. See, it's easy.

Photo Messaging

the future's bright, the future's Orange

orange

1 | 2 | 3 | 4
The imagery used by Orange emphasizes the values of the brand, ensuring customers are getting the most out of their phone and their mobile lifestyle. The idea of making "the future bright" is reflected in all of its designs.

REALIZING POTENTIAL

Microsoft has come a long way since it was first launched in 1975. Then it was a very product-centric company. Now its design values are intended to communicate the idea of "realizing the potential" of its customers, whether they are general consumers or international businesses.

Microsoft believes that it can empower people through effective and efficient software—any time, any place, and on any device. This shift in thinking has been reflected in the way Microsoft is presenting itself in each of its markets.

Furthermore, Microsoft is also trying to build "Trustworthy Computing" as a platform to increase customer trust through improved responsiveness, accountability, and predictability in everything the company provides. This shift of brand focus comes in the wake of several years of bad publicity about Microsoft's business practices, which culminated in the famous antitrust lawsuit in the United States (the ramifications of which are still being felt).

"Enabling people to do new things" is what is now translated across every aspect of Microsoft's interaction with customers, from the softer and more user-friendly design of Windows XP to incubating new products, integrating new customer requirements, and interacting more deeply with new and existing partners.

Microsoft has also created strong and powerful sub-brands—a sensible strategy and a move away from its unpopular and often divisive "monolithic" approach in the middle of the last decade.

1° of separation between the action and the reaction.

Brand timeline

1976
The trade name "Microsoft" was registered with the Office of the Secretary of the State of New Mexico.

1978
Microsoft established its first international sales office in Japan, ASCII Microsoft.

1981
Microsoft reorganized into Microsoft, Inc., with Bill Gates as President and Chairman, and Paul Allen as Executive Vice President.

1982
Microsoft announced a new corporate logo, new packaging, and a comprehensive set of retail dealer support materials.

1983
Microsoft introduced its full-featured word-processing program, Microsoft Word for MS-DOS 1.00.

1987
Microsoft acquired Forethought, the developer of PowerPoint, a leading desktop presentation application. Microsoft released Excel for Windows.

1989
Microsoft announced Office, the first general business software for Macintosh systems available on CD-ROM.

1993
Microsoft reported that the number of licenced users of Microsoft Windows totaled more than 25 million, making it the most popular desktop GUI-based operating system in the world.

150

7
Bill Gates, the founder of Microsoft, has been fundamental in changing the perception of the company from an uncaring monolith to a more innovative and agile group of small businesses. This shift was encouraged partly by the antitrust case.

1 | 2 | 3 | 4 | 5 | 6
The main sub-brands of Microsoft are developed based on the audience they address—Developer brands, consumer brands (such as the xBox, msn, hotmail, and so on), and ingredient brands (such as .net).

1995
The US Court of Appeal reinstated a 1994 antitrust settlement between Microsoft and the Justice Department that was rejected by US District Judge Stanley Sporkin in February 1995. Microsoft Windows 95 was made available worldwide.

1996
The Interactive Media Division was created, consisting of MSN, the Microsoft Network online service; games and kids' titles; and the information businesses formerly residing in the now-dissolved Consumer Division.

1998
Microsoft realigned its product groups to respond to changing consumer and market needs. The reorganization focused the product groups on investing in Windows with the goal of delivering simplicity and scalability, allowing businesses to maximize their competitive advantage through their "digital nervous system," and promoting the Web lifestyle. Bill Gates appointed Steve Ballmer President of Microsoft.

1999
Microsoft® Windows 2000 Professional, Windows 2000 Server, and Windows 2000 Advanced Server operating systems were released to manufacturing. Microsoft unveiled the vision for its next generation of software and services, the Microsoft .net platform.

2001
Microsoft announced the worldwide availability of Windows XP. The Microsoft xBox video game system was also introduced.

SPEED WITH CHARM AND STYLE

Faced with increasing competition, particularly from low-cost carriers, the objective of British Midland Airways had to shift if the company was to succeed. It could no longer be considered as a regional carrier—British Midland had aspirations to become a global airline.

The first stage was to create a new corporate identity, look, feel, and brand design that would work over the widest range of applications, and so unify the company's marketing activities. The brand design needed to be easy to use, aesthetically pleasing and cost-efficient.

British Midland's positioning is about being lively, agile, and active, as well as being crisp, modern, and understated. In addition to these ideals, British Midland also wanted to appear confident, welcoming, and engaging. Most importantly, British Midland changed its name to bmi, a conscious decision to move away from the negative connotations of being seen as regional and small, exactly what the name "British Midland" evoked.

The "sailing curve" is one of the cornerstones of the bmi identity. It is a visual representation of the concept of sailing, a concept that is intended to reflect the brand values of ecological friendliness, style, and charm. The

Union Flag, which features prominently on the tail fins of all bmi aircraft, aspires to reflect similar values, and may also "borrow" from the values associated with another class-leading airline, British Airways.

Everything in the "customer journey," from the logo and livery of the aircraft to the lounges, signage, uniforms, and cabin interiors, has been benchmarked against contemporary design values.

Brand timeline

1938
Air Schools Ltd., which specialized in flying instruction for RAF pilots, was formed.

1949
Following World War II, Derby Aviation was founded.

1953
Derby Aviation introduced its first scheduled service.

1959
Derby Aviation changed its name to Derby Airways.

1964
Derby Airways changed its name to British Midland Airways (BMA), and introduced a new company livery in blue and white.

1965
Transfer of operations to the newly opened East Midlands Airport.

1968
BMA acquired by banking and investment group, Minster Assets.

1978
BMA and British Airways (BA) agreed to route swapping.

1985
BMA became British Midland (BM) and changed its livery to red, white, and blue.

1995
BM became the first airline to offer a reservations booking service with payment over the Internet—CyberSeat.

1996
The new company strapline, "The Airline for Europe," was unveiled.

1999
The UK Civil Aviation Authority granted BM licenses to New York, Washington, Miami, and Boston from London Heathrow.

2001
British Midland announced the sale of its ground-handling business to The Go-Ahead Group Plc t/a GHI Group. British Midland unveiled its new corporate identity, company livery, and transatlantic product. The airline would now be known as bmi british midland.

1 | 2 | 3 | 4
At the heart of the new identity is the redesign of the logo, a more stylish typeface, and a new brand design system. In addition, all of the photography used by bmi is clear, simple, and striking.

2

153

5

11 february 2001

Mr. Peter Knapp
Landor Associates
Klamath House
18 Clerkenwell Green
London
EC1R 0DE
England

3

4

6

2002
bmi announced the launch of a new low-cost airline, bmibaby, based at East Midlands Airport.

5 | 6
Aspirational phrases such as "sailing through the air" are used across stationery and marketing to reinforce the brand message.

MEDICINE TO LIFE SCIENCES

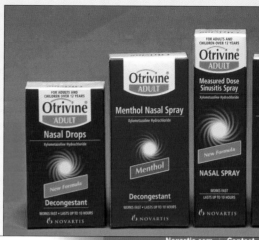

In 1996 two of the largest Swiss-based companies, Ciba-Geigy and Sandoz, merged to form a new pharmaceutical company. The creation of Novartis, the name of the merged entity, was at that time the largest corporate merger in history. The name is derived from the Latin *novae artes*, meaning "new skills." This reflects the company's stated commitment to focus on research and development.

154

The change in name heralded a change of focus for the business. With the approval of the US Federal Trade Commission on December 17, 1996, the last regulatory hurdles for the merger were cleared.

Since the merger, Novartis has created a uniform image for branded as well as generics drug. More importantly, Novartis has repositioned itself as a company in the business of health-care. It aims to improve the quality of life for people of the developing world.

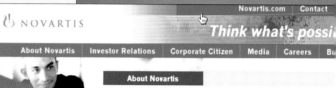

Brand timeline

1758
Johann Rudolf Geigy-Gemuseus began trading in various dyes and chemicals in Basel.

1857
Together with Johann Müller-Pack, Johann Rudolf Geigy Merian constructed a dyewood mill and dye-extraction plant in Basel.

1901
The name of the company was changed to J.R. Geigy Ltd.

1914
The company became a public limited company.

1859
Alexander Clavel sold his silk-dyeing factory to a new company, Bindschedler & Busch.

1884
Bindschedler & Busch transferred into a joint-stock company with the name "Gesellschaft für Chemische Industrie Basel," abbreviated to "Ciba."

1886
The chemical company Kern & Sandoz was created in Basel.

1918
"Interessengemeinschaft Basel" (Basler IG) was formed: an agreement between Sandoz, Ciba, and Geigy.

1928
Ciba took over of Geigy's production of textile auxiliaries.

1935
Geigy started to produce insecticides.

1938
A pharmaceutical department was founded by Geigy.

1939
A Geigy researcher discovered the insecticidal efficacy of DDT.

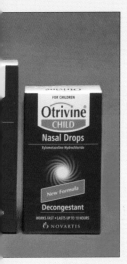

4

1 | 2 | 3 | 4 | 5
Novartis' mission is to bring value to patients and customers with the core values of external focus, innovation, and a concentration on people and performance.

5

1949

Geigy began manufacture of an anti-rheumatic drug.

1963

Sandoz acquired Biochemie GmbH in Kundl/Austria.

1967

Merger with Wander Ltd. and diversification into the dietetics business (Ovaltine, Isostar).

1970

Ciba and Geigy merged to form Ciba-Geigy Ltd.

1975

With the acquisition of American Rogers Seed Company, Sandoz was to move into the seed market.

1987

CIBA Vision was set up as a separate business unit.

1990

Sandoz was transformed into a holding company.

1992

Ciba-Geigy was renamed Ciba in line with the introduction of a new logo.

1996

Sandoz and Ciba integrated to form Novartis in one of the largest corporate mergers in history.

*Timeline Source:
www.Novartis.com*

NOVARTIS

| Novartis.com | Contact | Search |

Think what's possible

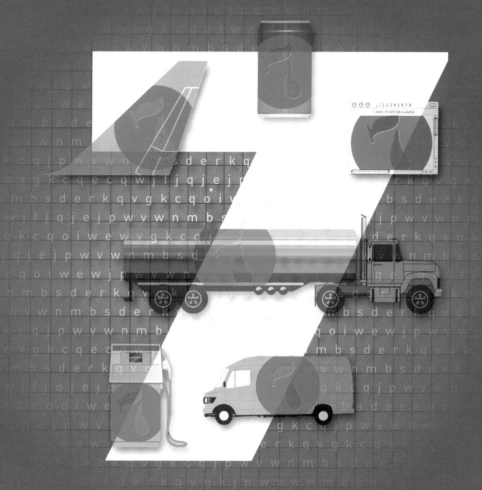

BURGER MEISTER

The success of McDonald's is based on an ethos of value, speed, cleanliness, and fun. These values have come to be represented in its "golden arches" logo, which has crossed language and cultural barriers to become a design icon. The logo is bright enough to remind children of its focus on kids' products, while smart enough to attract adults—whether or not they are parents.

The overarching "M" encourages visitors to enter and, wherever they are in the world, essentially they will find the same menu (although some products are subtly refocused for different territories and cultures), and the same design ethos of bright colors and clean information design.

Recently, the fast food behemoth has introduced its own take on popular dishes from world cuisine, indicating an awareness that even it needs to update its brand to keep pace with popular taste. This partial shift of focus has even extended to occasional TV advertising campaigns that are ironic rather than iconic: this megabrand has developed a sense of humor. It's saying, "We're not one of the bad guys; we can laugh at ourselves."

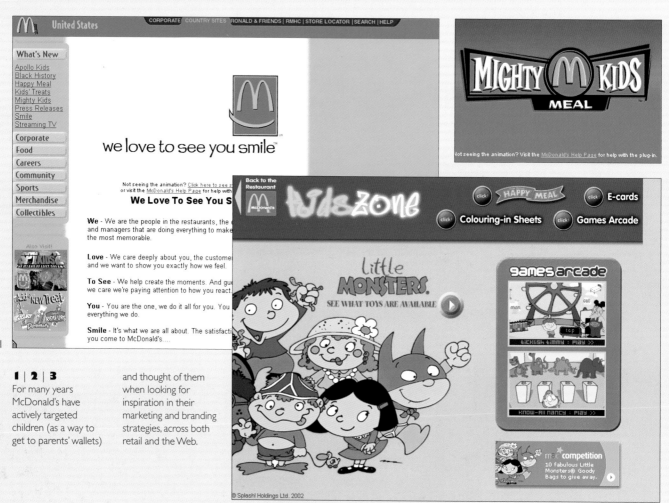

1 | 2 | 3
For many years McDonald's have actively targeted children (as a way to get to parents' wallets) and thought of them when looking for inspiration in their marketing and branding strategies, across both retail and the Web.

© Splash! Holdings Ltd. 2002

4

159

4 | 5 | 6
Continuous innovation
is the backbone of
McDonald's, and it
spreads across all their
products, ideas, and
campaigns. Recently
they have developed
menus that reflect
more of the culture
and tastes of a
specific country.

THE NEW McCHICKEN

PREMIERE

STARRING

SOUR CREAM
& CHIVE SAUCE

SALSA
SAUCE

CHICKEN
BREAST FILLET

FOCACCIA
BREAD

AT A McDONALD'S RESTAURANT NEAR YOU

5

Not seeing the animation? Visit the McDonald's Help Page for help with the p

McDonald's® Happy Meal®
Featuring
**SPY KIDS™ 2:
THE ISLAND OF LOST DREAMS**

6

FROM RUBBER BOOTS TO LIFESTYLE PHONES

Finnish mobile phone giant Nokia is seen as a benchmark of chic technology for the mobile generation on the move, but its origins are rather different. The Nokia Company originally ran a wood pulp mill, which was established in 1865. It merged with the Finnish Rubber Works in 1898, a company that made rubber boots and galoshes. In 1967, the corporate entity was an industrial conglomerate with four major business segments: forestry, rubber, cable, and electronics.

Nokia entered the world of cellular communications in the 1990s with the launch of its first GSM phone, the Nokia 1011. What sets Nokia apart from many competitors is a discreet brand design, coupled with an easy-to-use operating system and functional yet stylish hardware. In this way, the brand does not shout "Nokia," but leaves each new generation of phone to make its presence felt in a market dominated by flashy, trendy designs coupled with confusing operating systems.

That said, the company has designed some clever cobranding initiatives, most notably its tie-in with the Spielberg science fiction film *Minority Report*. The implied message: tomorrow's technology is here today.

160

1
Innovation and clever cobranding initiatives have made Nokia a powerful consumer brand.

2
Recent technological advances include WAP-enabled phones. Nokia promote the THR850 TETRA as a tool for helping professional users access crucial information from the Internet via their phone quickly and easily.

3 | 4 | 5 | 6
Other innovations just around the corner include the bluetooth car kit, which features a wireless headset, although recent laws may restrict the use of mobile phones in cars.

161

NOKIA
CONNECTING PEOPLE

Welcome to www.nokia.com!

Welcome!

Connect to the Future!
The summer blockbuster Minority Report is coming to Nokia.com. Check out the trailer, test your ethics, and sign up for a chance to win a Nokia 9290 Communicator in the USA or a Nokia 7650 in Asia-Pacific and Europe!

Mobile Phones
United States
  9290 Communicator
  Accessories
Europe, Africa, Middle East
  Nokia Next
Asia-Pacific

Games

Music

Home Products

Corporate Solutions
Nokia One
Secure Network Solutions
WAP for Mobile Business
M2M

Networks
Systems and Solutions
  3rd Generation
  Broadband Access
  Mobile Software
  GSM
  Public Safety
  Professional Services
Product Catalogue

Latest Press Releases

more...

July 31, 2002
Nokia provides MMS network solution to Optus in Australia

July 29, 2002
Nokia to further expand ONE's existing GSM 1800 Network in Austria

July 25, 2002
FTI Consulting Selects Nokia Internet Security Solutions

GPS for Nokia 9200 Communicator Series
Instant positioning, color maps, street and route finders... Enhance your Nokia 9210/9210i Communicator with the Nokia GPS Module and you're right on track. >>

Balance is a Beautiful Thing
Find balance in your busy lifestyle with the new Nokia 6610 mobile phone - equipped for business and styled for leisure. >>

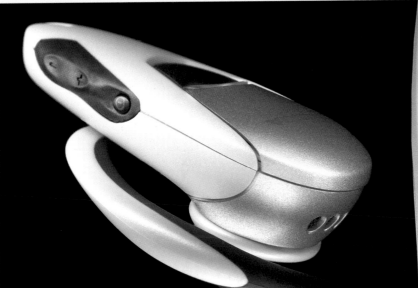

SYNONYMOUS WITH NEWS

The CNN logo is one of the world's most widely recognized brands, appearing on each of its news reports as a stamp of authority.

CNN first became a familiar global player with its "branded" news reports from the frontline in the Gulf War. People saw that the company was taking risks, and they saw the logo. By the time the first reports had come in from the frontline, CNN's brand values had been transmitted to the world.

Rather than redesign or update its visual identity, and potentially create a confused message, CNN has,

like MTV, changed the context in which its logo appears. For network trailers the CNN logo is animated over a series of energetic backgrounds to convey the vitality and technology of the network. At other times of day, or for specific programs, the logo appears against a variety of different images, textures, colors, and soundscapes that reflect the mood, tone, and nature of the programming.

In this way the familiar logo remains in the forefront of viewers' minds, but the fact that it is flexible ensures that it doesn't become obtrusive and inappropriate.

1 | 2 | 3 | 4 | 5

CNN's brand is carried across not just by its content, graphics, and the design of the various touchpoints but by the personality and attitude of its presenters who play a fundamental role in defining the brand's personality.

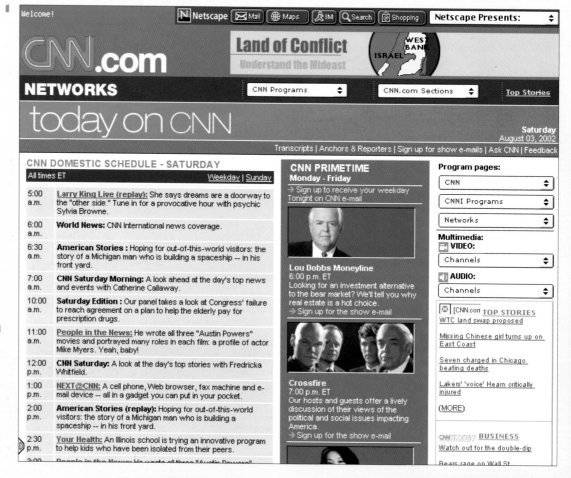

DO YOU YAHOO!?

The founders of Yahoo! chose the name because they liked the definition of a yahoo: "rude, unsophisticated, uncouth." "Yahoos" appeared in Jonathan Swift's novel *Gulliver's Travels*.

But the business created by them in their own travels is far from uncouth, although this type of branding appealed to Internet surfers who, as the medium took off, liked to appear alternative and countercultural.

Yahoo! Inc. is now a leading global Internet communications, commerce, and media company that offers a comprehensive branded network of services to more than 237 million individuals each month worldwide. The services all bear the brand's distinct look and feel, which says: color, fun, variety, innovation, and speed—coupled with trust, reliability, and an authoritative source of information.

One of the company's innovations has been to allow customers to create their own communities under the Yahoo! brand. So, by offering free services that allow people to publish their own passions, interests, and individuality for the world to see, Yahoo! can also adopt the limitless personalities of its customers by association. Ride 'em, cowboy!

164

2

YAHOO! Mail ✉

Welcome to Yahoo! Mail

You must sign in to read or

New to Yahoo!?

Sign up now to enjoy Yahoo! Mail

- Yahoo! Mail is FREE — sign up now!
- Accessible from any internet connection
- Plenty of FREE email storage
- Filter unwanted mail with SPAMGUARD
- You can also create a personalized email and domain with Personal Address

Sign up now

Learn more...

1

YAHOO! TV 📺

Yahoo! - Entertainment - Help

Inside Entertainment: Movies • Music • TV • Games • Horoscopes

Local Listings

Browse by Date & Time

Today Now Go!

Search listings by Keyword

Go! Advanced Search

So Real. So Ricki.
Ricki Lake
Weekdays

Yahoo! TV

Inside

Local Listings

Today's Picks

News & Gossip

TV Database

Nielsen Ratings

Soap Operas
provided by: SOAP CITY

TV Shopping

Today on Yahoo!

Welcome to Yahoo! TV

Features

Soaps by SoapCity
Get the daily dish from the web's largest & most popular soap opera information site.

TV Show Database
Get the information you need on all of your favorite shows!

Simon Baker is
THE GUARDIAN
TUESDAYS
9PM ET/PT

Today's TV Picks
Saturday August 3, 2002
- Big Brother 3
- She Spies: Poster Girl
- The Man With the Golden Gun
- Planet of the Apes
- Big Night

1 | 2 | 3 | 4

Yahoo! have designed their interface to be simple and clear while using the emotions of excitement and friendliness in the design. The most striking aspect of their branding is that, whatever service you choose, whether it's the local listings, mail, shopping, or business, the interface looks almost identical. You know where you are with Yahoo!

3

YAHOO! SHOPPING

Shopping Home - Yahoo! - Help

Four ways to shop: **Shopping** · Used · Auctions · Classifieds

Welcome, guest

My Shopping Account - View Cart - Sign In

Yahoo! Shopping

BACK TO SCHOOL

- Palm Student Offer from Palm Store
- HP Laptop from Wal-Mart
- Shop For It All from Macy's

What's New: 1.3 MP Canon Digital, $199 · Win a free bridal gown · Big Values on Home Décor

What's Hot: Design Your Own Jewelry · Bargains, Outlets & Savings · Xbox Only $199.99! · Sell Stuff

Find Products

[Search]

GODIVA
Chocolatier

▶ View our specially priced items
Savings up to 60%

FREE SHIPPING center
Check It Out

Featured Stores

Gateway

CDNOW

DELL™

babystyle MATERNITY * BABY

GAP gap.com

SONY

kmart.com

Mom's Favorite: Kmart.com

Strollers and bibs. Jumpers and mobiles. Besides a little sleep, every new mom needs plenty of help making baby happy. Give her a hand at

---

Help - Yahoo!

sting Yahoo! users
ID and password to sign in

hoo! ID: [   ]

ssword: [   ]

mber my ID on this computer

[Sign In]

de: Standard | Secure

help   Password lookup

**nail address you've always
d with** Personal Address

Powered by

Network Appliance™

e

Policy

4

YAHOO! Briefcase

Briefcase Home - Photos Home - Yahoo! - Help

powered by (hp)

Welcome, Guest

Options - My Folders - Sign In

Yahoo! Briefcase

Folders

You are not signed in. You need a Yahoo ID to use Yahoo! Briefcase.

New User

Sign me up!

Registered with Yahoo!

Yahoo! ID
[   ]

Yahoo! Password
[   ]

☐ Remember my ID & Password

[Login]

Trouble signing in?

Add Files
Import/Upload your files to the Web...

Share with Friends
Share your files with friends and family...

Announcements

Yahoo! Briefcase is still the easiest way to put your files online and share them with friends or co-workers.

- Get 30 MB of space, absolutely free
- Access your important files from anywhere
- Save Yahoo! Mail attachments directly to your Yahoo! Briefcase

Get more out of your Yahoo! Briefcase with Premium Storage.

- More Storage space! 50 MB for as little as $2.08/mo
- Share your files publicly
- Upload bigger files! Even larger presentations will fit

Connect to Briefcase from your Windows desktop with the **Yahoo! Drive Client**. Drag and drop or save files directly to Briefcase from any application. Download the beta version

RELATIONSHIP IS KING

Dell Computer is a classic example of the "relationship is king" model. Back in his dorm room in Austin, Texas, in the early 1980s, Michael Dell had an insight into a better way to build and sell computers. Rather than mass-producing his PCs and selling them through the retailers, Dell decided to bypass the channel and deal directly with customers.

This business model gave Dell two advantages. First, the brand could lower its manufacturing costs by tying these directly to the orders received. Second, and more important from a branding perspective, Dell established a direct dialog with customers, providing the feedback the company needed to continually serve customers better.

The result is a powerful—and valuable—relationship cycle. This direct connection has served as the cornerstone of the Dell brand in a crowded market. Where choice is overwhelming, people often opt for the brand design that says: "You can talk to us."

166

1 | 2 | 3 | 4 | 5 | 6
The philosophy of Dell is to keep their customers at the centerpiece of all their work and deliver value. In a crowded market where there are a great many players, Dell's philosophy resonates across their communication structure, from management values to the products themselves.

3

4

5

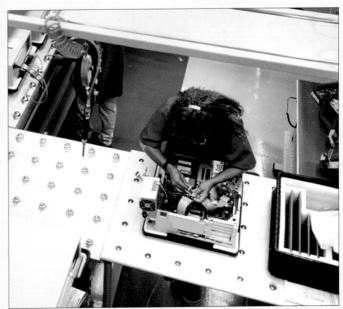

6

EVERYDAY LOW PRICES

In the small town of Rogers, Arkansas, Sam Walton founded Wal-Mart at the end of World War II. When the first store was opened it was meant to be nothing more than a single-unit outlet.

Sam Walton's passion for creating value for customers and "Everyday Low Prices" led to the creation of Wal-Mart's four retail divisions: Wal-Mart Supercenters, Discount Stores, Neighborhood Markets, and SAM'S CLUB warehouses. The retail design and planning of these different formats reflect the values and needs of the various customers.

In the years since then Wal-Mart has become a major force to be reckoned with, snapping up large retailers throughout the world and defining, for better or worse, what can and cannot be sold to a mass market.

But its brand design is everything: functional, no-frills layouts and information design that give the customers what they want, and tells them where to find it. The company has its critics, but its success amply demonstrates the power of upfront, unpretentious brand design that does what it says and nothing more.

1 | 2
Wal-Mart have managed to create a unique retail experience in their different formats by matching the implementation of the format to the target audience, from neighborhood stores to discount warehouses.

3   4

3 | 4 | 5 | 6

Everything about
Wal-Mart's stores says
function. Customers
believe that the savings
that Wal-Mart achieves
by keeping its stores
simple is passed on to
them. The primary color
schemes and solid, basic
use of typography
reflect the sense of
everything kept to its
most basic, and least
expensive, level.

5   6

A CENTURY OF INNOVATION

3M's success comes from its ability to provide unique and innovative solutions to its customers' problems. 3M was founded in 1902 by five businessmen who set up a mineral deposit mine for grinding-wheel abrasives. But the deposits proved to be of little value, and the new Minnesota Mining and Manufacturing Company (the three Ms of the name) quickly moved to producing sandpaper and other innovative products at the time.

The 3M brand with its distinctive red logo is a precious asset, as are Post-it, Scotch-Brite, Scotch, and Scotchguard. In 1977, 3M was chosen to become the umbrella identity for worldwide use across all its separate brands.

This proved to be a clever strategy. First, the company allowed its products to speak for themselves and become innovative solutions to everyday problems. Then the corporate brand moved into the foreground, and its products were subtly redesigned to appear under the

umbrella heading. Now 3M is a badge of quality and innovation that customers recognize when they are looking to make the "right" choice, even if they do not consciously look for the 3M brand. This trust is then transferred to other products.

1

2

3

4

171

5

6

1 | 2 | 3 | 4 | 5 | 6
3M's focus on both people and products has clearly positioned them as innovators in the market, be it light management, film solutions, fuel cells, or light fiber.

COCA-COLA—A BRAND AMONG BRANDS

From "The Pause That Refreshes" via "The Real Thing," to the simple "Enjoy," exceptional campaigns and classic design have helped Coca-Cola establish itself as one of the world's leading brands. Coke and Santa Claus (with a "Coke"-red tunic) are linked in the minds of many people in the West.

Coke's branding is an exercise in how it should be done. The basic logo has changed little in a century, yet the context of the logo has been subtly updated over the years. A Coca-Cola can remains forever a Coca-Cola can, but the 21st-century version is bright, reflective, and contemporary, while retaining all its definitive elements: the logo and the Coke red.

The Coke bottle was one of the original iconic packaging designs: a strategy imitated by dozens of companies, to varying degrees of success, ever since it first appeared.

172

1 | 2 | 3 | 4 | 5
The color, the shape, the fonts, the look, and the product itself have all lasted the test of time and competition in a way that most brands aspire to achieve—there is no other way to define what Coca-Cola has managed to achieve in a very difficult and competitive market.

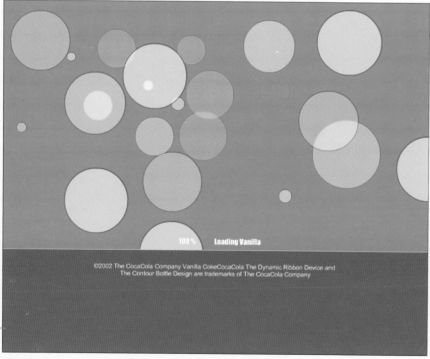

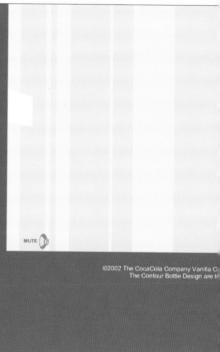

SHOP COUNTRY SITES CONTACT US SITEMAP

American Idol

Vanilla Coke

Youth Pa

HOME OUR COMPANY CITIZENSHIP INVESTORS PRESS CENTER CAREERS CONTACT US SITEMAP

Our Company
What's New
Our Beliefs
Our Diversity
Leadership
Our Brands
Around the World
Our Heritage
About Bottling

Coca-Cola

Supplier
Guiding
Principles
go there »

WELCOME TO COCA-COLA

The Coca-Cola Company exists to benefit and refresh everyone who is touched by our business. Founded in 1886, our Company is the world's leading manufacturer, marketer, and distributor of nonalcoholic beverage concentrates and syrups, used to produce nearly 300 beverage brands. Our corporate headquarters are in Atlanta, with local operations in nearly 200 countries around the world.

Our local strategy enables us to listen to all the voices around the world asking for beverages that span the entire spectrum of tastes and occasions. What people want in a beverage is a reflection of who they are, where they live, how they work and play, and how they relax and recharge. Whether you're a student in the United States enjoying a refreshing Coca-Cola®, a woman in Italy taking a tea break, a child in Peru asking for a juice drink, or a couple in Korea buying bottled water after a run together, we're there for you.

 2001 ANNUAL REPORT

VISIT OUR NEW
MYTHS AND RUMORS

INTERESTED IN
DOING BUSINESS
WITH US?

MORE TO EXPLORE...
» Principles Of
  Citizenship
» Press Center

4

rd your city/city

Dynamic Ribbon Device and
CocaCola Company

Vanilla Coke

reward your

MUTE

©2002 The CocaCola Company Vanilla CokeCocaCola The Dynamic Ribbon Device and
The Contour Bottle Design are trademarks of The CocaCola Company

5

SHARE MOMENTS, SHARE LIFE

With the slogan "You press the button, we do the rest," George Eastman in 1888 introduced one of the first basic portable cameras to the world. In so doing, he made what had been a cumbersome and complicated process easy to use and accessible to nearly everyone.

Through the years, Kodak has led the way with an abundance of new products and processes that have made photography simpler, more useful, and more enjoyable. Not every brand can achieve a strong connection with its consumers that will serve as the basis for loyalty for years to come, but Kodak has managed to do just that.

The Kodak brand has always stood for ease of use, quality and trust—and for the emotional experience of taking and sharing pictures.

The brand's color scheme and simple logo have extended Kodak's seal of quality over all of its photography-related services.

174

1 | 2
Kodak has become a word that signifies sharing, happiness, and innovation worldwide; a simple abstract word when it started has today transformed into a global force.

3

Kodak ADVANTIX Cameras

Perfect gifts for everyone

4

Kodak ULTRA

EKTANAR Lens

Tax free prices fro~~m~~

The Kodak Advantix gift pack makes the perfect gift. With 6 cameras in the gift pack range*, from £25.44 to £84.84 tax free, there's a perfect present for all your family and friends.

Each gift pack contains a Kodak Advantix camera, pouch, battery, Advantix film and a stylish picture frame to display your favourite shot, as well as a Kodak Picture CD Demo Disk.

*Selected models available at Dixons Tax Free include the T700, I520, F320 and C370. Kodak, Advantix, Kodak Ultra, Kodak Max and Share Moments, Share Life, are trade marks.

3 | 4 | 5 | 6
There is no doubt that the increasing popularity of digital photography has forced Kodak, a traditional, film-based company, to innovate and create. However, the Kodak brand has such resonance that few can doubt that the company's partial transition to the world of digital imaging will be helped by its familiar logo.

175

ADVANTIX T700 ZOOM
Kodak Picture CD
DEMO DISC
Kodak Picture CD

6

Kodak ULTRA max
36 EXP. FILM

5

JUST DO IT!

Nike, named after the Greek goddess of victory, was a setup in a garage. With such a "do it yourself" aesthetic, it's no surprise that the product is such an important part of what Nike is about.

Nike has extended that idea and turned it on its head; now the "Just do it" applies to the company's loyal followers, who feel they can adopt the freewheeling ethos by buying into the brand's values.

Nike's business is a truly aspirational one. Nike stands for excellence—and not just in its products. Nike's

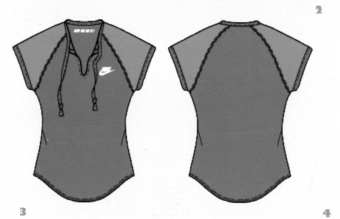

swoosh is a tick of approval for all of the high-profile achievers and sporting heroes who have adopted the Nike look as part of what they are about. The achievers wear the brand—and the brand wears the achievers.

Niketown in London and New York is the ultimate brand extension. For the faithful who visit it, it's like "coming home'; for the followers who don't, it remains a statement of what they are about, even if they don't acknowledge it. For nonbelievers, it's a shoe shop as a way of life. Either way, the company wins.

Online, the brand allows customers further in, by letting them customize a pair of shoes in their own chosen colors. The price is high, but for people who buy in wholesale to the sports and clubbing aesthetic, their name on a famous shoe buys them a place with the stars on the walk of fame.

177

5   6

1 | 2 | 3 | 4 | 5 | 6
Making shoes and sportswear a lifestyle is not an easy task. However, in spite of the very demanding customer base, the tough competition, and the need for a huge range of products, Nike clothing and sportswear today remain the most highly prized to their target audience. The company reflects all that is good in sports—success, endeavor, strength, and determination.

DOUBLE SKINNY LATTE TO GO

Jerry Baldwin and Gordon Bowker, whose interest in coffee stemmed from wanting to enjoy a good cup of it, founded the original Starbucks in 1971. However, Howard Schultz truly maximized the brand's potential when he joined as CEO in 1982 and created new standards in the business.

Starbucks is more than just about coffee: it's about brand design writ large, turning a near-commodity product into a complete experience on every street corner.

The key to the brand's uniqueness is that Starbucks has created its own vocabulary in the coffee-drinking world. Getting customers to live the brand to such an extent that they change the way they ask for a coffee is no mean feat.

Cafés used to be about finding a good cup of coffee in a good location in which to talk, relax, read, and watch the world go by. Starbucks has stuck its label on that way of life, and has bought the street corners and the coffee beans to supply it. The experience remains the same, but you wear the label and speak the language, even if you don't realize it.

And if you like Starbucks coffee, you know you can find it wherever you go. Want to design a brand? Try chasing the Moby Dick of coffee, Starbucks.

3

your account | help | checkout | sign in

STARBUCKS.COM

shop online | our stores | starbucks card | in grocery | for business | about us

buy a card
reload your card
register your card
large business orders

powered by hp

search

go

Starbucks CARD

A Starbucks store in your wallet The Starbucks Card offers the convenience of shopping online and in participating Starbucks locations with one quick and easy payment method. Use it to purchase anything from our online store or breeze into your local participating Starbucks to pick up your favorite beverage without worrying about cash. Starbucks Cards make great gifts – pick one up today!

Summer shade Our collection changes with the season -- find a perfect gift.

Sweet refreshment

Check your balance Already have a Starbucks Card? Enter your card number and PIN to check your balance.

card number

PIN

go

tools

• Buy a card

• Reload your ca...

• Register your ...

• Business Gifts... Orders

Creating an experience not only through the right retail planning but also by atmosphere, and of course the right products, is what has made the Starbucks experience special for its customers. So supremely confident are they that you'll visit time and time again that they have even made a Starbucks card available for use in any Starbucks of your choice.

179

4

bscribe Our newsletter livers the latest from arbucks.com.

ter email address

Job Center Find your future at Starbucks.

Starbucks Summer Catalog Request a copy.

5

PREMIUM BRANDING FOR THE MASS MARKET

Walkers, the UK market leader in potato chips, realized that they are not just for a youth or family market. They recognized that flavor is a key reason for consumers choosing a brand and so they developed a new range for adults, Walkers Sensations.

Landor, global branding consultants, designed the packs for Walkers. The inspiration for the imagery was to suppose that the potato chips had been handmade by a celebrity chef. The design, colors, and images were created with a focus on provenance.

In recent years Walkers' simple, color-coded branding has been subverted by the company to powerful effect, swapping the colors normally associated with flavors. Bringing in former UK and international soccer star turned TV presenter, Gary Lineker, was also an intelligent move. His "nice guy" image was subverted by the brand; it was a sign that here was a brand prepared to play with people's expectations and turn everyday snacks into something more appealing to adults.

1 | 2 | 3 | 4 | 5

In a very commodity-led market, creative thinking can make a significant opportunity. This is what Walkers proved by introducing a new brand to cater to the adult market. Walkers Sensations have created impact not just by innovation in flavors but by comparatively sophisticated merchandising and displays.

180

2

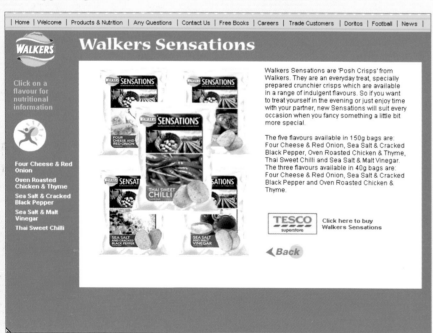

1

3

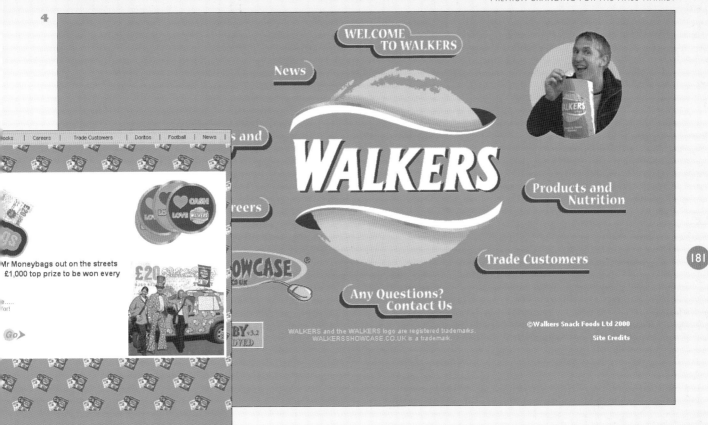

Mr Moneybags out on the streets
£1,000 top prize to be won every

.....
fort!

Go ➤

sponsored the England U15s squad. (That's where Michael
vement and commitment to the development of football at
d dramatically.

y using well-known footballers to star in our commercials.They
the naked Romario streaking across the pitch and soccer star
Lineker's ear. Of course, we have had Gary as a nun, a baby,

the famous Walkers sun logo on perimeter hoardings at all the
Snack of the England team as well as the sponsors of the
Leicester City fan , you will know in the past we have been the
cester City Youth Academy.

Walkers Football Fund Mini-site

More infor
Walkers Yo
Academy

The official
the England

Walkers an
England U1

Walkers an
Schools

11 October 2002

News home page

Walkers Youth Aca

City legend Gary Lineke
food giants Walkers ple
support to young Leice
and fans of the future.

Leicester City FC and W
unveiled Walkers Snack
new sponsor for its Yo
Junior Foxes member

The Leicester based fir
been involved with the
than 11 years announce
City's training ground
Gary Lineker and Acade
Oakes.

The five-year deal mea
continue to have prese
including appearing on

Walkers Celebrate
Queen's Coronation

Walkers Crisps have provided
their very own dedication to
the Queen's forthcoming
Jubilee celebrations, by
creating a brand new flavour
of Walkers Crisps -
Coronation Chicken flavour.

You will have to move quickly
as they are a special limited
edition and won't be around
long! They are in the shops

LENNOX v LINEKER - The Final Blowdown

Wednesay 31st of July saw the latest Walkers ad hit our TV screens, starring none other than Gary
Lineker and Lennox Lewis. In a battle of the giants the heavyweight champion of the world Mr Lennox
Lewis comes face to face with Walkers Wimp, Mr Gary Lineker and guess what, it was no contest!

Click here now for Exclusive Behind the scenes footage, The TV AD and Exclusive behind the scene
photographs.

Click here to find out about the new ad   Go ➤

KEEP ON RUNNING

Land Rover is one of the leading brands in the 4x4 vehicle sector, and its history is a testimony of innovation and off-road design excellence, from the original Land Rover, which was launched in 1948, to the current models.

The current Land Rover model range encompasses the Defender, Discovery, Freelander, and Range Rover. Each is a unique, yet no-nonsense vehicle ideally suited to the requirements of its clients. The new product line is a mix of British opulence, stylish shape and design, and top-of-the-line capabilities. Range Rover has been reinvented and its classic shape improved for the 21st century.

Even though changing and updating design is a much more complicated process for a brand like Range Rover, it is now in its third stage of design development. The latest Range Rover has combined modern appearance

with proverbial chic, such as the clamshell bonnet, horizontally split tailgate, and upright front end. Longer, taller, and wider than the previous model, the new Range Rover has more space and a stronger on-road presence.

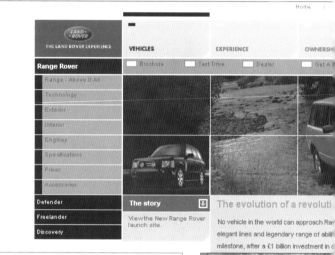

1

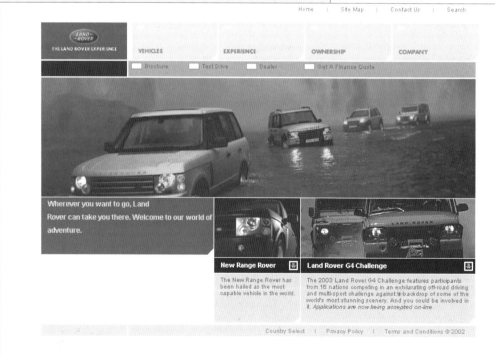

2

THE LAND ROVER EXPERIENCE

3

4

5

1 | 2 | 3 | 4 | 5
Designing the right
product and brand is
not just an important
matter for retail brands
in food and drink; it
applies to all products
that involve the
customer emotionally.
Land Rover knows this
well and hence has
updated its product
line to meet its
demanding customer
base.

184

GLOSSARY

ad banner A still or animated graphic object found on a webpage, used to advertise a product, brand, or company. Banner ads are still among the most common form of advertising on the Web, and come in a variety of shapes and sizes.

banner A graphic image, acting as an advertisement, that typically runs across the top of a webpage or sits in a designated ad-space. Banners usually conform to particular physical dimensions, file size and file formats.

brand The physical and emotional concept by which a specific product or service is readily recognizable. Brands are symbols, logos, names, or trademarks (or a combination of all four), and their purpose is to instigate or reinforce a relationship between the customer and the product.

brand advertising A form of advertising that is designed to create a favorable image of a brand and its full range of products and services, rather than of a particular product.

brand attributes The perceptions, deliberate or otherwise, that a brand creates in the minds of its customers. Different people will respond in various ways to a brand, depending on their socioeconomic circumstances; the same brand attributes, therefore, can create negative or positive associations.

brand architecture The implementation of a portfolio of brands. Most commonly it defines the relationship between corporate brands and sub- (or spin-off) brands, or a corporate brand and its main products and services.

brand audit A comprehensive, primarily financial review of the equity relating to a brand. Although a financial report, the value of a brand often bears little relation to a brand's profitability. For example, the Amazon brand, although having one of the highest perceived values of the recent dot.com ventures, has only just begun to return a profit.

brand awareness A measure by which target consumers can recall a particular brand. There are two major categories of brand awareness. "Unaided awareness" is the spontaneous identification of a particular product; "aided or prompted awareness" is when brand can be identified from a list.

brand equity Both the perceived (also known as 'reputational collateral') and real value that a brand adds to a particular product or service.

brand essence The fundamental characteristic by which a brand can be defined.

brand expansion The technique used to expose a brand to a wider customer base. This can be achieved either physically, by geographically extending the brand's availability, or emotionally, by subtly altering the brand to appeal to a broader section of people. Its purpose is ultimately to increase sales.

brand extension The utilization of a brand on products or services for which the brand was not originally created. Certain brands have such strong recognition and identity that they can be used successfully to market other products. An example is the use of the Porsche brand to sell products other than cars, such as clothes, sunglasses, and watches.

brand identity The deliberate and positive associations that a brand strategist wants to impose on a particular brand. Brand identity is key to instigating the relationship between the brand and the consumer and reflects the essence of the brand. Brand identity should not be confused with brand image. The former is the active strategy of how the brand owner wants the brand to be perceived, while brand image is how consumers perceive the brand.

brand image The associations and perceptions that consumers have about a particular brand. The brand image reflects the current relationship between the product and the consumer. Brand image differs from brand identity, which is the perception that the brand strategist wants to create in the customers' minds.

brand loyalty The strength of preference for a brand compared to other similar available options. This is often measured in terms of repeat purchase behavior or price sensitivity.

brand management The strategic management of a particular brand in order to maintain or increase brand equity. Brand management involves designing brand identities, monitoring brand effectiveness, and making any appropriate alterations to the brand identity, if deemed necessary.

brand personality The image or identity of a brand expressed in terms of human characteristics, such as young, old, warm, etc. Identifying a brand's personality helps target consumers to relate more closely with the brand.

brand positioning The "market space" occupied by a particular brand. Considering brand positioning helps identify over- or under-subscription of a certain market by the competition.

brand slogan An instantly recognizable phrase that recalls or reinforces a particular brand. "Don't Leave Home without It" effectively helped consumers to associate American Express with travel.

brand strategy The overall strategy created by a brand owner or the designated management team to make the brand as effective and efficient as possible, thereby improving the brand equity.

brand value The monetary premium that is gained from having customers loyal to a particular brand and who are willing to pay extra for it.

brand valuation The process by which the value of a brand (or brand equity) is calculated. This will include the "good will" value as well as the brand's revenue.

browser An application that downloads content from a server on the World Wide Web, then interprets and displays it to the user in the form of webpages. The most widely used browsers are Microsoft's Internet Explorer and Netscape's Navigator. There are differences between the way that browsers display webpages.

button A clickable graphic, commonly used to load a new page or execute some other instruction. In some cases, buttons can be used as adverts.

cobranding A method by which two brands (constituent brands) that share either a common brand position or complementary product create a product (a composite brand) that carries both brands.

consumer brand The term used to describe the brand identity of a specific product or service that a company or corporation offers to (noncorporate) consumers.

copy The words that accompany the visual elements of an advertisement. Copy is generally used with brands that either have a complex message, a high-tech specification where words (i.e. the spec) can sell, when the message is abstract, or when slogans are key to the brand's message.

corporate brand The term used to describe the brand identity of an actual company or corporation (such as Mercedes or Unilever) as opposed to a specific product. Corporate brand can also be used to describe a service offered to other businesses.

e-commerce Business transactions conducted across the Web. This area of Web design is very specialized and requires in-depth understanding of secure protocols and financial transactions technology.

guerrilla marketing Any marketing method that does not use conventional techniques.

hyperlink An embedded link between text, pictures, buttons in a webpage, and other parts of the site or another website. Sometimes called a "hot link."

image attributes Those elements that help to define the tone, manner, personality, and style of a firm brand, very often the differentiating factor between similar service firms.

intellectual property branding A form of branding that relies on specialist knowledge and expertise. Examples of companies that might use intellectual property branding are legal and financial companies—companies that need to be perceived as knowledgeable, trustworthy, and professional.

interstitial A commercial advertisement that appears between two webpages on a website, taking over the entire browser window before forwarding the user to their original destination. This forwarding must take place within five seconds.

logo The words, letters, and/or symbols that, together make up the physical brand of a product. Most logos are pictorial representations of the brand's product or service. Some logos will also feature a motto or phrase.

mood board Visual representations of a brand's identity. It may show color palettes, fabric swatches, typography, and any other element that embodies the product.

naming matrix In branding, a matrix that illustrates the conceptual positioning of a brand name. Names fall into four categories: emotive, abstract, inspirational, and descriptive.

passion branding A form of branding in which the product generates strong desires and drives. Similar to aspirational branding, passion branding works well with companies such as Ferrari and Rolex.

pop-under A Web advert that appears in a separate window beneath the browser window, where it is hidden until the user closes, moves, or resizes that window.

pop-up A Web advert that appears in a separate window on top of the browser window, usually disappearing after a limited period. A pop-up may contain text, graphics, links, or animation.

push-and-pull media Term used to describe the two main forms of media. Push media, generally speaking, refers to broadcast media, such as radio and TV. This form of media simply outputs the programs, and consumers have a choice either to watch or listen or not. Pull media refers primarily to interactive media, such as the Internet. Here users dictate what they want to see.

relationship branding A form of branding that relies heavily on a "one-to-one" relationship with the consumers. Relationship branding usually involves personalization, whereby an individual customer's details are kept and regularly updated. Amazon, for example, keep records of a customer's previous purchases and use a cross-referencing system on their database to suggest other titles that may be of interest.

retail brand Name given to the branding used in retail outlets. Although shop or store space will vary from premises to premises, the interior design must still accurately reflect the corporate brand.

service brand Name used to describe a specific service product, as opposed to a tangible product.

skyscraper A common format for Web-based advertising; a tall, thin box that usually appears at the side of a webpage.

superstitial Unicast's interstitial ad format. A superstitial is cached by the browser before playback, and must be of set dimensions (550 × 480), length (20 seconds), and file size (100Kb).

surfing The act of searching for material on the World Wide Web.

targeting The practice of purchasing advertising space on particular websites with the aim of reaching a specific audience for a specific campaign.

touchpoints Term used to describe any region of interaction between a brand and its target consumers. Advertising, point of sale, and customer care are all examples.

transit advertising Any form of advertising that appears on moving objects, such as buses, taxis, and supermarket lorries.

URL abbr.: Uniform Resource Locator. The unique address of a webpage on the Web, consisting of a resource type (www), a domain name (company.com), and a page locater (home.htm).

values branding A form of branding that utilizes specific values, a way of life, or a philosophy to promote its message. Nike and Disney are two good examples.

viral marketing An Internet ad campaign, the success of which relies on individuals sending material associated with the product, either a game, animation, or video, to a number of friends, who in turn send it on to more friends.

INDEX

189

ACKNOWLEDGMENTS

Accucard Ltd.
Adidas
Admedia
American Express
Avon Cosmetics

Benetton
Borders Group Inc.
BMI
British Tourist Authority

Candy Spa. Italy
CC logo copyright Chanel Ltd.
Clear Channel
Coca-Cola
Condé Nast
Creative Club

Daimler Chrysler
Dell Computer Company
Diageo Company Ltd.
Dyson

egg
Eli Lilly
E.M.I.
E.M.A.P
Evian Danone Waters

FedEx
Financial Times

Glaxo Smith Kline

Harrods
Heinz
H.M.V.
Hoover
Hoover Candy Spa. Italy
H.S.B.C.

Ikea
Intel

JetBlue Airways

Kelloggs
Kimberly-Clark
Kodak
Kraft Foods Europe

Labour Party
Landor Associates
Levi Strauss

3M
McCann-Erickson
Microsoft
MUJI

Nestlé
Nike
Nokia (UK) Ltd.
Novartis

OgilvyOne Worldwide
Oracle Corporation
Orange

Parfums Jean-Paul Gaultier
Pets.com
Pifzer
Procter and Gamble

Royal Warrant Holders' Association

Sainsbury's Supermarkets Ltd.
Sellotape Company (UK)/Henkel
Shell
Sky Active Shopping
Sony
Starbucks Coffee Company UK Ltd.

Tesco
Turner Broadcasting

Unilever

The Virgin Group
Volkswagen (uk)
Volvo Cars

Wal-Mart
W.H. Smith